# Combat He Wrote!! - The Amazing True Story of "Combat" Hudson

By

Ross R. Olney ©

ISBN 978-1-3002866-4-6

## Dedication

By Charlie "Combat" Hudson

*To my wife, Mary, who endured all my reckless*

energy, never making a single complaint in our
forty-nine years of marriage. Her patience and
understanding allowed me a lot more freedom than I
deserved. She spent most of her life raising our
two fine sons Terry and Steve. Her dedication
humbles me, and now I am aware that I should have
tried harder.

By Ross R. Olney

To all the combat flyers who know it is true when I
say we all felt fear. Not so much of getting
killed, but rather of getting maimed, or blinded,
or horribly burned, or of having our balls shot
off. Which is why we sat on our helmet, right?

## Contents

Chapter One      Mission Number Four
Chapter Two      The Beginning
Chapter Three    Becoming a Bombardier
Chapter Four     Exact Opposites, 1 and 15
Chapter Five     Missions 2 and 3

| | |
|---|---|
| Chapter Six | Manny Klette and Other Heroes |
| Chapter Seven | Good Guys, Bad Guys, Mistakes |
| Chapter Eight | The End of the Conflict |
| Chapter Nine | Charlie Hudson Day |
| Chapter Ten | The Great White Animal Hauler |
| Chapter Eleven | The REAL Animal Hauler |
| Chapter Twelve | The Great Breakout, and More |
| Chapter Thirteen | Yet Another Adventure |
| Chapter Fourteen | The Final Test, I Only Hope |

## Chapter One   Mission Number Four

"Christ! That hurts!"

I swore it out loud that October 9, 1943, to anyone on the airplane who would listen. I could hear myself speaking over the howling of the wind blasting through the jagged hole in the skin and shattered nose cowling of the B-17 "Lightning Strikes." Charlie Hudson never thought much about that kind of pain before, but I was hurting like hell. You could have shoved a silver dollar through the bloody, irregular hole in my left wrist where steel had ripped in one side and out the other, mangling the flesh and shattering the bone. My left shoulder was also throbbing with agonizing waves of pain and streaming blood where another hunk of Nazi iron had torn in.  My right arm above my elbow had taken some shrapnel as well.  I could see blood soaking through both sleeves of my leather flight jacket.

"<u>Damn</u>!" I said, but this time I'm not sure if I spoke aloud.  Was I afraid?  Yeah, I guess so.  I've said many times since then at lectures, "In combat, if you weren't <u>afraid</u>, you weren't <u>there</u>!"

Funny, but as bad as it hurt, I could still function.  Maybe the human body recognizes when it's in serious trouble, when it's near the end.  It fights back.  At least with some people, it does.  Maybe my body knew that it couldn't just lie down and doze off, that if it took that tempting route we were dead.

I tried to collect myself, to resist.  "Settle down, Charlie," I advised softly.  "Take it easy. We're not gone yet.  We're hit, we're hurt, but we're not dead...and the Krauts are still out there, still trying to kill us."

The cold wind screaming through the holes in the bombardier's compartment in the nose of our badly crippled bomber helped to clear my mind, to focus on the problem. Fighters were still coming in from the air and the instant they pulled back anti-aircraft gunners would resume

blasting away from the ground.  They had determined our
exact altitude and you could have parked the airplane on
the steel layer of flak around us, it seemed so solid, when
they started again.  I felt a chill rush through me as I
looked out at the falling, smoking, burning B-17's, the
falling German fighters, and the falling bodies of friends
and enemies.  There were also many floating parachutes of
the luckier ones from both sides.  Our two wing airplanes,
squadron friends who had been flying on each side of us,
were gone, shot down in flames.  We were trained to count
parachutes, to report the number at the post-mission
critique to help determine who may have lived and who may
have died, but on that day it was impossible because there
were so many.  In fact, Bo Gabler, one of my best buddies,
was out there somewhere.  Bo had gone through training with
me and back then, years ago it seemed at that moment, we'd
made a deal.  We'd wave to each other as we floated down
into Germany on parachutes.  Bo was in one of the wing
airplanes that took a direct hit.

      "I _swear_ that guy was waving at us as he dropped
out of the airplane," said a voice over the intercom.  I
looked across and saw a chute open.  It had to be Bo, for
he still seemed to be waving up at us.  Years later, after
the war, I located him.  He'd spent several of those years

in a German stalag, a prisoner-of-war camp.  I asked him
about the wave.

"Hell, yes, that was me waving at you, Charlie. I
said I'd wave at you, and I did."

Fighters screamed around above us in the clear
sky, their iron crosses plain on the sides of their
fuselages. I took a deep breath, ripped open my uniform
sleeve, and administered a dose of morphine from my kit.
In seconds the soft warmth of the drug in my blood spread
to my shoulder and arms, and down to my bloody wrist.

The pain subsided somewhat.

They hadn't really told us about this back in
Bombardier School at Williams Field in Arizona, but what
the hell, I had to do something.

"Charlie?"  The voice snapped over the intercom.
It was Captain Bud Evers, the pilot of "Lightning Strikes,"
our fortress in the flight.  "Charlie, are you OK down
there?" he shouted.  The bombardier's position is forward
and a few feet lower than the pilot's, down in the
greenhouse-like nose with the navigator.

"I'm hit, Bud, but I'm OK.  I'll do what I can,"
I said with all the confidence I could muster.

"Roger, Charlie.  Understand."

If I thought things were bad then, they got much

worse.  Before the mission was over, Bud Evers and co-pilot
Bob Roberts hand-carried that bullet- and flak-riddled
Flying Fortress back to England by sheer will power and
tremendous flying skill.  They seemed to hold the Fort in
the air with their hands on the controls, and their will
power.

"<u>Fighters</u> at <u>nine o'clock</u>!" snapped over the
intercom.

"<u>More</u> of them at <u>twelve o'clock high</u>!" yelled
another voice.

We had been under constant fighter attack - even
a few heavier Stukas joined the party - for three hours and
forty eight minutes.  The Stukas, normally dive bombers in
the Luftwaffe, were trying out a brand new "grenade
launcher" device mounted on their wings.  They would streak
through one of our formations, grenades flying out to each
side.  The tactic didn't work too well, but along with
everything else, it was nerve-wracking.

It was also possible, and it did happen, for
highly trained B-17 waist gunners, in an attempt to hit a
German fighter inside the formation, to machine gun and
even destroy one of our own Fortresses.

If the Stukas and the other German fighters
weren't enough, the instant they streaked away the terrible

flak began again. We were nearing the target. Lightning
Strikes, our fortress, had managed to avoid most of the
coastal guns, a difficult task since some of them were
mounted on railroad cars and very difficult to track. But,
nearing the target, we were in a flak field that was
deadly.

Not that this was all that much different from
other Flying Fortress bombing missions over Europe. It was
my fourth bombing run from our base at Bassingbourn,
England, and the first three had been bloody messes as
well. I'd known from the beginning, from when I applied
for flight school, that casualty rates were high on B-17
bombing missions across the English Channel. But I
remember looking forward to combat. I remember wanting to
get in the fight, wanting to do my part to win the war. I
was young then and I wanted to blast that miserable little
Adolph Hitler and his cronies to hell.

I was finally in the fight, for sure, and in
spades. I was up to my neck in it. Mission number four, a
combat flight I'll never forget, was actually screwed up
from the start. First of all, we were promised Royal Air
Force Spitfire fighter cover, we called them "Spits," but
it was to be "high" cover at forty thousand feet. B-17's
normally flew combat missions at around twenty thousand,

and this mission was to be even lower. So we all got a
real laugh when they announced this RAF Spitfire
"protection" at briefing.

     As I forced my throbbing left hand around the
stock of the gun in the nose turret of Lightning Strikes to
prepare for another flight of approaching German fighters,
I realized I was lucky to be there in the first place.  I
should have been dead already, and it should have happened
shortly after our take off from Bassingbourn.  I was very
lucky not to be cold and dead in the icy North Sea below.
Here's why.

     We were the first B-17's from a base in England
to use an additional fuel tank mounted in the bomb bay for
longer runs.  The huge spare tank supplied extra fuel for
take off and climb out then, when it was empty, it was to
be dropped into the North Sea.  That was the plan of the
experts who didn't have to fly these missions, and in this
case it seemed like a good one.  Fuel from the B-17's wing
tanks was then used for the bombing run and the return
home.       The Focke-Wulf airplane factory at Anklam,
Germany, 75 miles from Berlin, was the target for this low
level mission number four.  It was to be a very long
flight, so we were using, for the first time, one of the
extra bomb bay fuel tanks.  At first the mission was

routine, and we did conserve wing tank fuel by using fuel from the drop tank. We didn't know it, but we were in the calm before the storm.

After draining it dry, the extra tank should have been no problem. The airplane could easily handle the temporary weight of the extra load of fuel, and I figured the tank was a blessing. It could be dropped anytime. Unfortunately, when the time came to drop it over the North Sea, I discovered that the big container wouldn't electrically jettison as the designers had promised. Something had gone wrong in the circuit wiring.

Still in good physical shape at that point not long after takeoff, I wasn't that worried about the problem. Bud Evers called to ask if I could get rid of the huge tank mechanically. Hell, the Army Air Corps had a strategy for everything, even a situation like that. I knew what the standard operating procedure was and, in fact, looked forward to the challenge. It was the bombardier's job to go back to the bomb bay and manually release the tank.

"Can you do it, Charlie?" Bud's voice came over the intercom. "We need to get rid of that tank."

"I'll take care of it, Bud," I told the pilot confidently. I knew what to do. Unhooking my oxygen tube

and intercom, I opened the bay doors electrically then
crawled back to the bomb bay.  The North Sea drifted along
beneath us, much closer than I'd ever seen it before.
Stacked in a rack opposite the empty fuel tank were the
bombs for the upcoming mission.  Wind was howling and
buffeting around in the bomb bay.  Moving as carefully as
possible, I inched my way along the narrow steel catwalk by
the fuel tank.  There was a safety chain stretched
lengthwise from one rib to another, and it was on this
chain you had to stand and balance, leaning across the top
of the tank, to reach the release mechanism on the wall of
the bomb bay.  With wind snapping and pulling at me, I
climbed up on the wobbly chain, braced myself, then looked
across the top of the spare fuel tank to the far bulkhead
for the manual release. It was a rather prominent screw the
airplane factory had built in for just such an occasion.
They promised that the screw would, with one quarter turn,
release the heavy tank to drop free.  I could just reach it
by stretching out with my screwdriver, my feet wobbling on
the chain.

        Even though I was new at this tank release
business, I wasn't stupid.  Standard operating procedure is
to hook your chest parachute harness strap to something
solid before you lean out of an airplane door or over an

open bomb bay.  Most crewmen wore the harness, but stored the chute near their position in the airplane.  Then, in case of trouble, they could quickly snap the parachute to the chest hooks on the harness, and be ready to bail out. My chute was up in the bombardier's station in the nose, but I was wearing my harness.  I found a spot on what I thought was the bulkhead rib support, hooked up the chest chute harness strap with the steel clip, then, feeling relatively secure, leaned over the fuel tank and tried to turn the screw with my screwdriver.

The damned thing wouldn't budge.

Every fighter plane in Germany would soon be approaching, and I had to get back to my guns and my bombsight in the nose.  We didn't have time for this nonsense.  I reached out with my heavy-handled screwdriver and whacked the screw hard.

Nothing.

I hit it again, then again.  The tank didn't move.

To <u>hell</u> with it!  I reached over and <u>beat the shit</u> out of the screw.

The tank <u>still</u> didn't drop.

By then I was getting dizzy from lack of oxygen. At any altitude over 10,000 feet you can begin to feel a

need for oxygen, especially when you're working as hard as
I was to get that damned screw to turn. I could feel
myself getting dizzy, and although I figured I couldn't
fall out of the airplane even if I passed out, I certainly
didn't want to be dangling up there on the end of a strap,
banging around in an open bomb bay with hard metal corners
and brackets digging and jabbing me in the buffeting wind,
all while I'm unconscious. I knew I needed oxygen, so I
reached over to unhook my chest chute harness strap.

Then I did nearly faint. I'd hooked the strap
not to a solid bulkhead on the airplane, but to a strut
holding the temporary fuel tank in place. If the tank had
dropped, so would the strut have dropped, and so would
Second Lt. Charlie Hudson have dropped, far, far down into
the cold North Sea below. Of course, I wouldn't have felt
the cold, and that was at least something. Even if I'd
been wearing my parachute, it would have done no good under
the circumstances. If I'd had one, and if I'd had the
presence of mind to open it, it would have instantly ripped
away with the heavy weight of the tank to which I'd
strapped myself pulling us to the rough water below.

Breathing heavily from fear as well as lack of
oxygen, I worked my way back to the radio compartment where
I picked up a walkaround bottle of oxygen.

"Ask Charlie what the hold-up is?" Bud Evers
yelled over the B-17's intercom to the radio operator. The
operator relayed the message to me.

"Tell him I'm on it!" I shouted. Evers had his
hands full. No sense bothering him with my problem,
although I was still weak from the thought of what almost
happened.

Crawling back to the bomb bay, I re-hooked my
chest chute strap, this time to a very solid bulkhead on
the ship. Then I crawled up on the swaying chain and,
steadying myself on a cross beam, reached out again with my
screwdriver. With the blade in the slot, expecting
nothing, I twisted the handle.

As God is my witness, with the gentlest twist of
the screwdriver, the temporary tank suddenly released and
dropped into space under the airplane with a great howl. I
watched it tumble down toward the choppy North Sea, stunned
by how easily the drop mechanism had worked.

But, OK, the tank was gone. Hands still shaking
a little, I cranked the bomb bay doors shut with four or
five good hard turns of the manual mechanism. This could
have been done electrically from the front, but I still
wanted to steady myself. Then I started forward, back to
my own station in the nose. The Focke-Wulf factory at

Anklam was waiting, and we had a full load of bombs. To
this day I don't believe Bud Evers, the pilot and my long
time friend, knows what happened to me in that bomb bay.

My problems with murderous Mission Number Four
had just started. I didn't know it then, but I was going
to lose a lot of blood on that mission.

And I was going to kill a man.

A B-17, a "precision" bomber, normally dropped
its bomb load from at least 19,000 feet or higher, but it
could be done, and done well, from nearer the ground. Our
orders on this mission were to drop from a much lower
altitude. Evers continued on to the target, our B-17
roaring along far lower than usual until I was certain that
a German soldier on the ground could have shot us down with
his sidearm.

At the very last minute, before we had a chance
to drop our bombs, we took a direct anti-aircraft hit into
an engine and it immediately burst into flames. With fire
flickering back across the wing, Bud Evers had no choice
but to shut down the engine and feather the prop. This did
blow out the fire but it also effectively painted a big red
sign on the side of our ship, a sign that said LOOK AT ME -
I'VE BEEN HIT - I CAN'T FLY AS WELL to every German fighter
plane in the sky. With three engines, Evers managed to

maintain our altitude and hold us in formation, but we knew
we would very slowly but surely become a "sitting duck."

Our situation continued to deteriorate.  We were
deep in Germany with only three engines on a B-17 full of
holes.  The sky outside was filled with German fighter
pilots desperate to win their Iron Cross by shooting us to
the ground.

We just wanted to drop our bombs on the target
and fly home, in that order and as quickly as possible.

Some pilots would have aborted the mission. They
would have ordered the bombs dropped on some remote German
meadow or hamlet this side of Anklam and turned for home.

Bud Evers?  Are you joking?  Not only did he want
to stay with the formation for as long as possible, but he
was a pilot who always wanted to hit the target.  Nor did I
want to become known as a "Chandelier," which is what they
called a bombardier who had to drop his bombs on a
worthless target, or in the Channel.

We were OK so far.  The fire was out, we had
three good engines, some good gunners, and, I figured, a
good bombardier.  We had a full load of bombs, and enough
fuel to make a run and then get home.  We'd fought off
fighters before and we were close to our target.  We were
at 12,000 feet when I finally released the bomb load over

Anklam, scoring several direct hits.  Except for constant
harassment from German fighters away from the target, and
the usual heavy anti-aircraft fire from the ground over the
target, the mission appeared as though it would turn out to
be a rousing success.

Hell, I was a bombardier.  I'd already dropped my
bombs and hit the target.  My job should have been over,
except to scare off some fighters.

It was just beginning on mission number four.

Waiting in my station in the nose, I grabbed the
handles of the twin 50's and blasted away at every fighter
in range.  Lightning Strikes was handling relatively well,
shot up as she was and on only three engines, and we were
beginning to feel pretty good about the whole thing.  The
wild beating of my heart from the near disaster in dropping
the spare tank had subsided, and I was almost enjoying
myself.  My guns actually began to glow a cherry red from
rapid firing.

Then we took the hit from the fighter who got me.
I was thrown violently against the back wall of the
bombardier's compartment as bullets ripped into the nose of
Lightning Strikes. For a split second I was stunned as my
body rolled around among the spent shell casings.  At that
instant another chunk of steel from the same fighter ripped

through my wrist.  Blood poured from the wound.

The horror story that circulated back in bombardier school suddenly began to make sense.  Back then, they told of the guy on the ground crew whose only job was to hose down the inside of combat B-17's following a bombing mission.  That is, after recognizable body parts had been removed.  Only then did I begin to understand.

Many times after that day I've wondered if the flak or the bullet would have ripped into my head if I hadn't been on the floor.  Or, if I had been at my guns, would it have missed me altogether?  Do combat crewmen who are wearing their steel helmet worry more about taking flak in the ass, or, if they're sitting on their helmets to protect the family jewels, as many do, might they then worry more about getting their head blown off?  I'll never know.  I only knew I was in serious pain.

It really hurt!

"How bad are you hit, Charlie?" asked Lightning Strike's navigator, Bruce Moore, as he helped me up.

"I don't know, Bruce.  You take the guns and keep the Krauts away from the front of the airplane," I shouted.

"What's going on down there?" yelled Bud Evers.

Moore shouted back, "Charlie is giving himself a shot of morphine; I'm trying to get out of the way!"  With that, he ducked between some heavy boxes of ammunition, shouting something that sounded like "We're screwed! We're screwed!"

"Get on that gun!" I bellowed, and he did. My shout seemed to clear his mind, and he was quickly back in the fight. I completed the administering of the shot of morphine to myself. With my Mae West jacket strap as a sling for my left arm, and with cold wind whirling around in the nose, I returned to the machine guns and began firing. Moore took up his assigned cheek gun on one side of the nose or the other, depending upon the fighter's line of attack. All the time I knew we were falling further and further to the rear of the formation, back to what most crews called "Purple Heart Corner," and thus attracting more and more fighters. German pilots had been trained to concentrate their fire on wounded bombers out of formation, bombers lacking protective fire from their wing mates.

Another flak burst tore through the nose station of our badly damaged B-17, and I was thrown to the floor again, this time on my back, my feet over my head. A piece of this flak had torn into my shoulder. But I had no choice. I scrambled back to the guns and fired the final few rounds at an approaching fighter who wanted one more shot at us. This turned him away at the last moment. While

I waited for more ammunition, another small sliver of flak ripped into my right arm above the elbow. I was being cut to pieces, slowly and with precision. Both sleeves of my flight jacket were soaked in blood.

With yet another self-administered shot of morphine, I could feel the pain fading. The crew back in the rear began throwing overboard everything that wasn't fastened down. They knew they had to lighten the ship to keep it in the air, especially since the last burst of flak had torn into one of our three remaining engines, and it was failing. German farmers must have wondered at the shower of metal and GI issue material falling from the sky, including heavy machine guns, ammunition, safety equipment, radio apparatus, jackets, and other loose gear of any kind. If we had any bombs left, we were supposed to drop them on the coastal Frisian Islands, the location of a German fighter base, but we had none, and we were too busy to worry about that anyhow.

Slumping down in the nose section of the battered airplane, I waited for the drug to continue its work. At that instant, through my port window, I saw two rapidly approaching JU88 fighters. They were coming straight at us from the Islands. One veered off toward another straggler, the other came directly at the nose of struggling Lightning

Strikes. Immediately Bud Evers began what evasive action he
could manage with the injured B-17, but the JU88 pilot
continued on his attack run.  The German pilot fired too
quickly, missing us completely.  I remember thinking in my
haze that he had to be new at his job, or farsighted.  It
wasn't important.  Though he didn't know it, the German had
little time left because I had a final ace up my sleeve.
The crew had sent up one last can of ammunition before they
began to lighten the ship, passing it forward to me like a
long snake, from waist to radio operator, to co-pilot, to
navigator to my station, stretched out down the length of
the airplane until I got it collected in the nose station.
My guns, the only ones on the ship since the others had
been jettisoned to lighten the plane, were loaded and
ready.  Waiting for the return of the JU88 in our crippled
B-17, I watched the French coast pass beneath us.  We were
limping along only 75 feet or so over the water of the
English Channel. I thought we were low before, when I
dropped the spare fuel tank and bombs, but we were really
low by then. By hand signal up through the plane, I knew
when the JU88 was coming in to attack.  The tail gunner
waved at the waist gunners, they waved to the radio
operator, he signaled the pilot and finally the wave came
to me.  The German was coming in from the rear.

"Bud," I called to the pilot.  "Can you steady the plane?  I think I can get this guy."

The German and I fired at the same time as he approached, but we both missed.  "Bud," I screamed, "hold her <u>steady</u>!"

The fighter swept around and approached from the rear again. I heard the tail gunner yelling, "Hit 'em hard, Hudson, hit 'em <u>hard</u>!" as he signaled forward.

The German pilot streaked his sleek JU 88 over us from the rear, then he shot out in front, rising.  I don't know why he did that.  He must have thought we were out of ammunition.  Maybe he was setting us up, figuring we were helpless. Maybe he wanted to attack from the front, as enemy pilots often did.

What was written in <u>Target: Germany</u>, billed as the Army Air Force's "official story" of the U.S. bombing of Europe, was as follows.  "There never was - then or now - any question about the reckless, almost suicidal courage of the German fighter pilots."  I agree with that assessment, having seen many German fighter pilots in the heat of combat.  Still, even though I admired him a little, I stitched the belly of the reckless German's JU88 from nose to tail with my twin 50's, watching as the heavy bullets ripped up through the cockpit and killed him.

Chunks of airplane dropped off.  He never knew what hit
him.  The sleek JU88, streaming smoke just like in the
movies, gently banked to the left, turned over slowly, and
smashed into the water in front of us.  Lighting Strikes
roared through the spray that erupted when the German plane
hit the water below.  I could feel it showering through my
flak-torn canopy, hitting me in the face with its
refreshing coolness and soaking my bloody flight jacket.

It felt damned good!

"You got the son of a bitch, Charlie, you got the
son of a bitch!" I heard Bruce Moore shouting, all the time
pounding me on the back.  I was so full of morphine it
didn't even hurt.  Funny thing about morphine, you feel
very sharp mentally, sharper than you ever felt before, but
physically things don't seem to work the same.  You just
don't seem to give a damn.  Everything moves much more
slowly, as in a dream.

Mission Number Four, one we considered a suicide
mission from the start, struggled on to Bassingbourn barely
above the water.  At one point before or after my kill, Bud
Evers went below to crank up the bomb bay doors since
Lightning Strikes' electrical circuits had long since
failed.  At that moment co-pilot Bob Roberts had to take a
violent evasive maneuver to avoid some fighters. Evers flew

to the roof then crashed back down onto the four inch bomb compartment catwalk with a scream, straddling it one leg on one side and one leg on the other, the narrow steel walkway between. Certain very vulnerable parts of Bud were temporarily crushed, later swelling to several times their normal size. Evers had trouble walking for two weeks, painfully hobbling about the base. We flew on.

Even then, when we should have been safe at home, mission number four didn't end calmly. Far from it, in fact. We were just above the water of the Channel, and our course, as we crossed into England, carried us directly over Cambridge University and on to Bassingbourn eleven miles further inland. We couldn't really maneuver and it didn't appear we would clear the towers and steeples of Cambridge we were so low, so Bud Evers fired up the damaged engine for extra lift. The oil quickly caught fire again, but we began to climb slightly. I'll never forget it, and neither will the young English students with beanies and bow ties staring up at us as we thundered across their old school. We cleared the steeples by a few feet, then Evers shut down the damaged engine again. The fire went out as he feathered the prop. Bassingbourn was just ahead.

As we made our final approach and lowered our landing gear, we found that one of our wheels had been

blown away.  It, too, had probably landed on a German farm
house, or at least I could only hope so.  Bud Evers ordered
the entire crew to assemble in the radio room, then belly-
landed the 24 tons of maimed metal on the hard runway.

I've never heard a plane land without wheels -
from inside, that is - and I learned that it is very noisy.
The tortured skin screams against the concrete, the roar is
deafening, and the stench of friction-burning metal and
rubber and plastic sears the nostrils, almost choking you.

By then in shock from my injuries, I leaped from
the airplane the instant it stopped and ran wildly back up
the runway, temporarily avoiding the fleet of ambulances
racing forward.  We were the only plane from our squadron
to return from Mission Number Four, and I was certain, in
my haze, that Lightning Strikes was going to get me in the
end by blowing up in a great boiling mass of flames.

One of the ambulances caught up with me, loaded
me aboard, and rushed me to a field hospital at Diddington.
For many years since the war I've been a professional
golfer, a career I was hoping for even then, so obviously I
was worried about my left arm.  As I lay waiting among many
other wounded men I heard the docs talking about cutting
the arm off.

"Bullshit!" I roared through my morphine haze,

"You ain't cutting off _my_ arm!"

Doctor Buffington, one of our flight surgeons who years later owned a clinic in Garden City, Kansas, entered the discussion. I heard him say he thought he could save my arm, so he went to work. I was awake all the time.

"Move your little finger," he would order right there in surgery, and I would do it. That would allow my brain to tell him through muscles still working which tendon was which in the bloody hole above my wrist.

"Now move your thumb," he would order softly.

He stitched together tendons, then went up and brought bone down and grafted pieces where the worst shattering had occurred. Finally he put a cast on my arm for a couple of weeks, then he began to graft skin. I may not be the greatest golf pro today, but I made golfing my career and I play a pretty mean game. The docs did a good job on both my arms. It took them four months, but they got it done. I still think of them and mentally thank them every day. It would be difficult to swing a golf club with one arm, though I guess it has been done.

I also believe that pilot Bud Evers, who had just reached his _nineteenth_ birthday and within one year would become the oldest surviving pilot in the squadron, and co-pilot Bob Roberts, should have received the Distinguished

Service Cross they awarded me for that rugged mission over Anklam, on the day we blasted a Focke-Wulf plant to hell. Those two pilots managed to fly our shattered B-17 home, an almost impossible accomplishment, and that, to me, deserved the great honor of a DSC, one step below the Congressional Medal of Honor - if not the Medal of Honor itself.

## Chapter Two     The Beginning

Back in my youthful oil field days in Taft, California, back in my early twenties, I had no idea Hollywood would one day make a gritty, audience-pleasing motion picture called "Memphis Belle," and captivate a whole new generation of movie fans with the danger of B-17 bombing missions over Europe. Of course I had no idea back in those days that I would be flying bombing missions over Europe, or, for that matter, looking down and seeing monkeys looking back through an airplane instrument panel, or that I would be working on a true prison-escape movie with famous actor Charles Bronson. Nor did I have any idea that in the future, in 1944, by my fourth bombing mission over Europe, I would be featured in the popular "Strange As It Seems" column in newspapers across the country. There

would be a large drawing of me in uniform between a drawing
of a mangrove tree (explaining that mangroves never drop
their fruit) and a drawing of a strange-looking device
(reporting that Bell Labs had developed an electrical voice
and ear for telephone testing). Under the drawing of me,
author John Hix would say that 1st Lt. Charles S. Hudson, a
flying fortress bombardier, was cited for heroism on three
of his first four bombing raids.

I never suspected any of this, but it all
happened.

"Memphis Belle" was an electrifying and quite
successful movie about one B-17, her young crew, and about
how they made it through the required twenty-five-mission
tour of duty over Europe. On its "final" mission over the
heart of Germany, the part of her life the motion picture
covered, the B-17 Flying Fortress called Memphis Belle was
machine-gunned by German fighters and hit by German flak
(Flieger Abwehr Kanonen) and generally shot to hell. The
B-17 Memphis Belle had every possible thing happen to her
that could happen. Her crew, who arrived at their airplane
for their final mission singing "Amazing Grace," was
wounded and scared and emotional and even psycho.

But the Belle made it and the brave crew made it,
with some wounds, and we were all glad.

"They had the <u>heart</u>, the <u>courage</u>, and a <u>B-17 Flying Fortress</u> that would make <u>HISTORY</u>!" shouted Hollywood.

In many ways the film was pretty true to life, if you condense everything. Flying bombing missions was often very dangerous, and the <u>real</u> Memphis Belle had her share of tough combat missions. She and her crew served gallantly, with distinction and even heroism taking the same chances we all took, but no bomber, not one of mine and not the Memphis Belle, ever had all that happen to it all at once, all on one mission like in the movie. What didn't happen to the Memphis Belle in the motion picture happened to other planes on the Hollywood mission, in full view of the Belle's supposedly frightened young crew of actors. Other planes exploded, and collided with the enemy, and disintegrated in the air. The motion picture Memphis Belle took many hits, had crewmen seriously injured, and made it home by the barest of margins in the rousing finale of the exciting motion picture.

In fact, <u>none</u> of it happened to the <u>real</u> Memphis Belle, though in life they did fly some of the roughest missions of the war. The Belle was just one of the luckiest B-17's in the Army Air Corps. The real Belle never got hit, never shot down an enemy plane, and generally had a routine set of missions over Europe, if you can call bombing Europe "routine." Other planes fell all around her while the Belle cruised on, surrounded by flak though never taking a hit. But she was there, and that counts for more than something, it counts for everything.

Many of our missions, especially the later ones when fighter escorts had a longer range, were somewhat less harrowing. A few bombers like the real Memphis Belle were charmed, and rarely got hit at all, or rarely endured persistent fighter attacks.

But not, according to Hollywood, the amazing Memphis Belle.

Of course I didn't know it back in the oil field days in Taft, but out of the several rugged things that happened to the motion picture Memphis Belle and her crew on that last mission, at least three of them would be stolen from us, from me, and they really did happen. What the movie people did was tell the "story of the final mission" of the first crew to finish twenty-five missions (the Memphis Belle) then pile on everything exciting or tragic or brave that happened to many other B-17's, including our B-17 Flying Fortress.

You'll read later in this book how I slid the scalp of a gunner back into place and fastened it down with

a strap from a Mae West jacket.  That appeared in one cut
of the Memphis Belle movie.  You'll read about our two
frozen gunners and my three hundred sixty degree turn over
a target, all three of which appeared in Memphis Belle, the
movie.  The turn, leading hundreds of other B-17's, was
over a strategically-important railroad bridge, not a city
with a school nearby as they had in the movie. But we did
do it, and we all took twice the flak and twice the fighter
attacks to blast the target. According to the movie, these
adventures happened to the very busy Memphis Belle on her
last, fateful mission, before she and her crew went home as
heroes to sell war bonds - which I did later, so no
jealousy is involved here.  Movie people probably borrowed
other adventures from other planes as well, since the
record will show that the "Belle" did have a pretty tame
life.  The thing is, the daughter of director William
Wyler, a man who flew as an observer on the Memphis Belle
back when he was younger and making a documentary, decided
to make a feature film.  Wyler had saved several reels of
action involving that airplane and crew, shot from the
ground and in the air over the target, during the making of
the documentary.  So, naturally, when his daughter became a
movie-maker, she wanted to make a film using her father's
footage.

The result was "Memphis Belle," not a bad movie, really, if you understand that it was Hollywood and not real life.  For example, some time later one of the crew of the Belle was lecturing to an audience in Yonkers, New York, on the exploits of the by-then famous Flying Fortress.  He got to the part about the gunner with the skinned-back scalp and calmly told the audience that he merely skidded the scalp back in place.

"Wait a minute!" came a voice from the audience. It was the voice of B-17 belly gunner Leith Kerr who, sadly, returned to combat and finally died in action.

The speaker stopped.  "Yes...?" he called.

"I don't know what _else_ you did on the Memphis Belle," said Kerr, by then strolling down the aisle in anger, "but you didn't do _that_."

Flustered for just a moment, the speaker answered, "Why, what do you mean?  You saw the movie, didn't you?"

"Yes, I saw the movie, but it was Major Charlie Hudson who put back the scalp.  I know, it was _my_ scalp. See, it's almost healed," he said, grabbing his hair.  The audience roared with laughter and applause, and the rest of the lecture, I understand, went rather poorly.

Wyler wasn't the only "celebrity" to fly missions

with some of our B-17's.  The biggest male star in
Hollywood in the forties was macho heart-throb Clark Gable.
After the death of his wife, Carole Lombard, Gable joined
the Army Air Corps and as an officer was stationed with the
508th Squadron, 351st Heavy Bombardment Group, 1st Air
Division, Eighth Air Force.  He was there to make a
recruiting film, not to fly combat.  In fact, Hollywood
<u>forbade</u> him to get anywhere near flak or bullets, and his
superior officers agreed. But Gable, always a risk-taker
with motorcycles and airplanes and boats, quietly flew
several combat missions with his squadron.

My oil field days?

Working as a roughneck in an oil field and
fighting as a pro boxer may not exactly qualify you to be
involved in a Mexican prison escape that eventually wound
up as another motion picture, but why not?  Dancing around
the rotary table of a drilling rig didn't prepare me for
the algebra and geometry of the life of a bombardier,
either, but that's how I started as a young man, and I
don't think it hurt me a bit.  I was a fair student in high
school, and an outstanding athlete.  I lettered in
football, basketball and golf at Taft High School and Taft
Junior College.

We had a very efficient water boy on the Taft

High School football team back then.  He was too small to
be on the team as a player, but he loved the game of
football.  So he participated in the only way he could, and
he worked very hard at his job of delivering water to us
during time-outs. He would run quickly out on the field
carrying bottles, and move just as quickly off when the
time-out ended. Years later, in England, we bomber crews
were invited across the base to a reception at a fighter
squadron.  They were very proud and were celebrating the
fact that one of their pilots had on that day achieved a
"triple."  He'd shot down <u>three</u> German planes in <u>one</u> day.
I was at the bar, looking around for their guest of honor.
Finally the bartender pointed him out, down at the other
end of the bar.  I couldn't believe my eyes.

It was Gordon Graham, our Taft football team
water boy.  We rushed together and embraced and had a
wonderful, nostalgic conversation.  I was so damned <u>proud</u>
of him.

Gordon eventually became a Lt. General in the
United States Air Force.

But it was an event on a golf course that became
one of the most important incidents in my life.  I really
love the game of golf, and I suppose becoming a golf pro
had bounced around in my head, along with many other

things.  But I was really too young to be very serious
about a career.  I did spend as much time on the course as
possible. One day I was between caddy assignments.  As
usual, I was practicing on the driving range.  A Catholic
priest noticed my swing and approached me.  His name was
Father John Powers.

"That's a great swing you have, son," said Father
Powers, "but if you'd try keeping your right elbow a little
closer to your body, it would be even better."

What did I have to lose?  I held my elbow in on
my next swing, and the ball sailed fully twenty yards
further down the range than any other shot that day.  So
began a friendship that resulted in my becoming Father
Powers' personal caddy, and afforded me endless hours of
wonderful instruction from a superb golfer.  Father Powers
also provided me with money and transportation to be
tutored by Olin Dutra, the 1934 U.S. Open Champion.

Before long I was winning amateur golf
tournaments in Los Angeles at Hillcrest, Inglewood, Bel-Air
and Fox Hills country clubs.  And, sure, by then I <u>was</u>
thinking about becoming a pro on the PGA tour.

But I had also done some boxing in high school,
with fifty amateur fights and a good record.  In 1932 I
gave pro boxing a try.  I fought as a welterweight for

three years, with eleven wins, one loss and one draw. It
was at the Dreamland Auditorium in Oakland, California,
that I finally fought Joey Peralta for my one loss. I
remember it clearly to this day, and I can visualize the
row of angels they used as decoration in the auditorium.
Joey hit me so hard that day that when I began to come to
and saw the angels looking down, I thought I was in Heaven,
not Dreamland. That, in fact, ended my budding career as a
boxer, but really, the trouble with both boxing and golf
was that neither could provide me an immediate living. I
might have made a fortune down the line somewhere, but what
I needed was a regular income.

        The early 1900's weren't easy times. Dad was a
partner with Wyoming Governor Brooks in a cattle ranch.
Our brand was the Half Diamond L. It was a huge ranch, but
when the sheep came in there was a big hassle. The
Governor was a died-in-the-wool, if you'll pardon the
expression, cattle man, and my dad didn't mind sheep at
all. So they broke up the partnership. Dad took a vast
flock of sheep and the Governor took the cattle. Both did
well enough, but in time Dad's flock was hit with hoof and
mouth disease and thousands of our sheep died. Dad had to
sell his saddle and his own horse and everything else to
get us to a new life in Taft, in the rich California oil

fields.  He was always a good provider for my mother, my
two sisters, three brothers and me.  He went to work for
Standard Oil.

Under the instruction of Orville Hall, my oldest
friend and "second father," I took on a job as an
apprentice butcher, worked up to full butcher status, and
kept the job for five years.  I worked in most of the best
butcher shops in Taft, and in my spare time washed
airplanes for extra money and stick time.  Gradually my
life was forming.

I loved flying.

But, following in my real father's footsteps, I
went to work for Standard Oil when I reached my twenty-
first birthday.  They hired me as a roughneck in the Taft
fields of California.  The hours were long and hard, but I
liked the work, and eventually I was promoted to the
position of driller.  During my six years with Standard
Oil, I was often in full charge of men with many more years
of experience than I.  They were some of the greatest
people I will ever want to know, and I loved my job at
Standard Oil.

In every life certain things happen that may seem
minor at the time but turn out to be very major, like the
day I was on the driving range when Father Powers showed

up. My draft notice, arriving in May of 1941 while I was working for Standard Oil, seemed major to me at the time, as I'm sure it did to many thousands of other young men. I didn't really mind. I wanted to serve in the United States Army Air Corps as a pilot, and I planned to enlist anyhow.

But it was something less significant that turned my life around, and began some "right foot starts" in a career where starting on the <u>left</u> foot is important. Beginning on my right foot seemed to dog me throughout my life, and now that I'm a senior citizen and can look back, I'm very glad it did dog me.

Following the rules, I reported for my draft physical at old Doc Morris's office in Bakersfield, promptly at nine o'clock in the morning. The doc's clinic was a real mess, piled high with papers on every flat space including the examining table. Still, at the time, the condition of the office didn't seem very important. Doc Morris, I decided, was probably working too hard, treating too many patients, and neglecting his paperwork.

It became very important later, for while I was waiting, a rather pale-looking, sickly young man walked in and sat down next to me. I smiled and he smiled, so we began to chat. He told me he, too, was in for his draft physical.

I felt sorry for him.  Although I knew Uncle Sam was taking almost everyone at that time, my new acquaintance didn't seem physically equipped to handle battle situations.  It was impossible for me to imagine him in combat, in a foxhole.  I, myself, was in great physical shape, and I found myself wishing I could give him some of the confidence, physical stamina, strength and conditioning I'd gained from golf and boxing and oil field work.  We took our physicals, and I never saw him again.

In June my classification arrived.  What a shock! I was <u>4-F</u>!

Hell, that <u>couldn't</u> be!  I felt fine.  I felt <u>great</u>.  I <u>wanted</u> to serve.  I waited for them to straighten things out, certain in my own mind that old Doc Morris had mixed me up with the other guy, who was probably struggling through basic training as a 1-A, and just as confused as Charlie Hudson.

The problem was this.  I couldn't wait forever. The Army Air Corps didn't accept anyone over twenty-seven years old, and I was by then approaching that age.  With over 400 hours logged in single- and multi-engine aircraft, I had to <u>do</u> something.

So I simply went down and enlisted.

As was the custom, I was sworn in the next day.

Whatever might happen in the coming days, I was _in_ the Army
Air Corps at last.  When I passed the physical with flying
colors, I know for sure that the mistake had been made in
the disorganized office of Doc Morris.  To this day I ask
myself whether or not I should have called the Army and
told them about the other guy, and the mistake, but I never
did. After all, maybe he _liked_ the Army, and didn't _want_
them to know he was 4-F.  On the other hand, maybe he died
on some beach because he didn't have the stamina to go on.
I hope not.  I'll never know.

        It wasn't going to be the last time I started
with my right foot rather than my left on a great new
adventure. It was a military career that would bring me a
recommendation for a Congressional Medal of Honor.  I would
be awarded a Distinguished Service Cross, a Distinguished
Flying Cross with three clusters, several Air Medals, and
three Purple Hearts for injuries received in combat.  And
the Croix de Guerre from France, that nation's highest
honor.

        In June, 1940, German dictator Adolph Hitler
offered peace, under his own terms, to Winston Churchill,
Prime Minister of Great Britain.  France had fallen and
England was expecting an invasion any day. When Churchill
rejected the offer, Hitler ordered an all-out U-Boat attack

against British shipping with his strong fleet of
submarines.  This was a mistake, for it strengthened
British resolve.

Then, in September, 1940, on the advice of his
air force chief, Hermann Goering, Hitler made another bad
mistake.  This one was to directly affect Charlie Hudson.

The funny-looking but domestically powerful
little German dictator with the odd mustache ordered an
all-out assault on London by the German Luftwaffe.  The
Battle of Britain had been ongoing for some time.  But as a
result of Hitler's order to wipe out London, the Royal Air
Force's Bomber Command determined to strike back with a
series of retaliatory attacks on targets in Germany.  Since
this meant flying over enemy territory the moment they
reached the continent, the raids were necessarily long,
complicated, very dangerous and very costly.  British
bombers had to go in alone, since protective fighters
didn't have enough range to accompany them.  They had to
carry heavy fuel loads, thus smaller bomb loads.  Also, the
British had fewer long range bombers than the Germans, so
the damage done by the Royal Air Force was considerably
less than that being done to England by the Luftwaffe.  In
spite of these handicaps, there was a renewed feeling of
confidence among battered British citizens, knowing that

Germany was taking some of the same punishment being given them by the enemy.

Two types of bombing developed during the Second World War - strategic and tactical. Strategic bombing hit at the economy of the enemy, crippling his war effort by blasting his industrial production, his civilian morale and his communications.

Tactical bombing was air support of ground troops or sea forces.

I would eventually become totally involved with strategic bombing, of which there were again two types. One was "Area" bombing, directed at the industrial section of a city or, at times, an entire city. This was the method preferred by the night-bombing Royal Air Force.

The other type was "Precision" bombing, directed at very specific industrial targets such as a particular war production plant or a railroad equipment marshaling yard. A precision strategic bomber might from high altitude hit a ball bearing factory between two schools, blowing it apart without hitting either school. This, necessarily, was daytime bombing, since bombardiers had to see targets clearly through their very sophisticated (for the time) bombsights.

German bombers continued their attacks on London

under somewhat easier conditions. They were flying against
London from occupied France and the Low Countries and doing
very heavy damage. It was during this phase of the war
that Winston Churchill, speaking of the brave British
fighter pilots trying to defend London, said, "Never in the
field of human conflict was so much owed by so many to so
few."

Speaking of the high morale of the staunch, bomb-
shattered British people, Churchill also said during those
terrible days that if the British Empire were to last a
thousand years, "This was their finest hour."

When British bombers came in on German targets,
air defenses were strong, with fighter units and accurate
anti-aircraft weapons. So the Royal Air Force conducted
almost all of its strategic area raids at night, when the
planes couldn't be quite so easily spotted and shot down.
Royal Air Force "Pathfinder" bombers went in first, a job
for only the bravest crews who were especially trained in
night-target identification. Totally alone and vulnerable,
the Pathfinders dropped flares so the following heavy
bombers, who under the British system approached the target
one by one and on their own pre-planned headings (rather
than in American-type formations), could locate the general
area of the nighttime target. Gradually, the Royal Air

Force developed a very good night bombing system. Indeed, the raids became so successful that the British eventually cut back on the manufacture of fighter planes like the great Spitfire so they could increase long range bomber production. They were hitting Hitler where it hurt.

The United States entered the war in December, 1941, after the devastating Japanese sneak air attack on Pearl Harbor which almost destroyed the United States Navy in the Pacific. Along with Great Britain and other countries, we became the "Allies." Germany, and her weaker friend, Italy, quickly sided with Japan and became the "Axis."

Generally, at that time, the war wasn't going all that well for the Allies. England's Libyan advance had turned into a retreat. Germany's steamroller was moving forward toward Stalingrad. In the Pacific, Americans were making their last desperate stand on Bataan. The critically-needed British warships Repulse and Prince of Wales had been sunk by the German navy. Singapore was tottering. The Americans had no Navy left of which to speak.

In 1942, a lone Douglas airliner lumbered through the gray February dawn on its way from Lisbon to London. It was one of the most sought-after airplanes in the entire war. A solitary German fighter plane, one of a vast armada seeking to locate and destroy this airliner, flew into view above, but by an incredible stroke of luck, the unarmed airliner just happened to be out of sight under the wing of the German fighter. The young Nazi pilot missed his prey, the airliner completed its mission, and the entire war was changed.

Aboard and then relatively safe in England was the advance guard of seven high ranking officers of the newly forming American Eighth Air Force. They were carrying a directive from Army Air Corps Chief, Lt. General Henry H. "Hap" Arnold. It named one of the passengers, Brigadier General Ira C. Eaker, as American Bomber Commander in England, and ordered Eaker, my own future commanding officer, to "make the necessary preparation to insure competent and aggressive command and direction of our bomber units in England."

American leaders had conferred with Prime Minister Churchill and decided that of the three common enemies, Japan, Italy and Germany, the Third Reich, Germany, was the most dangerous. Allied leaders agreed to try to defeat Germany as quickly as possible, and one of the ways they decided to do it was by a massive strategic air offensive to destroy Germany's war production industries.  Italy, they felt, would fall quickly, either immediately before or immediately after Hitler, and the Allies could then concentrate all their forces on the Japanese in the Pacific.

All of these great political decisions were moving me toward one of the most exciting, dangerous times of my life.

General Eaker understood why the British were committed to night area raids, but he felt that daylight precision bombing was more accurate.  He felt that American airmen could successfully complete such raids without serious losses even though they would be without fighter protection for much of the mission.  This was a mistake on Eaker's part for the losses were staggering, but that was still the way we proceeded.  The United States had developed two new, fast, heavy, four-engined bombers, each equipped with enough machine guns and armor protection to be able to fight the Germans in the air and on the ground. One of these fast bombers was the slab-sided B-24 "Liberator," a mighty airplane.

The other was the awesome, magnificent B-17 "Flying Fortress," my airplane.

America had also developed the best bombsight in the world, the highly secret Norden bombsight.  It was a bombsight that would enable bombardiers like I was to become to make very accurate daylight strikes from high altitude.  It was felt by the experts that the accuracy of anti-aircraft fire would rapidly diminish the higher the gunners were forced to shoot.  This was wrong, it turned out, but the experts were sure that American planes would be relatively safe at high altitudes.  Planners had failed to take into consideration the skill of German anti-aircraft gunners on the ground, the quality of their weapons, and the reckless courage of German fighter pilots in the air.

In July, 1942, the first American bombers arrived in England.  As the brand-new and anxious to fight "Eighth Air Force," the all-American crews made the very first American raid on August 17, 1942.  This bombing mission blasted the railroad marshaling yards at Rouen, in occupied France, doing heavy damage with no losses.  By January, 1943, the Americans were making major raids against targets such as the German submarine pens at Wilhelmshaven.

The British press, which at first had been reserved in their comments on American bombers and crews, became enthusiastic.  They commented with amazement on the stamina of American flyers, men who were apparently unaffected by high altitude.  The Evening Standard, in a

thoughtful editorial, suggested that all the young American
airmen were "husky specimens" able to handle high altitude
without fatigue "because they were always playing
baseball."

A British doctor flew on some B-17 missions to
study the effect of high altitude on American crews. He,
himself, passed out, and the legend of American stamina
continued, greatly enhanced.

By June, 1943, American strategic bomber forces
were strong enough to start the long-planned "Combined
Bomber Offensive" against Germany.  It had become obvious
that American daytime "precision" and British nighttime
"area" bombing worked ideally together.  One publication of
the day said, "...the pattern of the rapier thrust by day
and the bludgeon smash by night began to emerge clearly.
It began to look as if Germany, having sown the wind, was
about to reap the whirlwind."

Massive daylight air strikes by American B-17's
and B-24's against Hitler's war industry, and massive
nighttime air strikes by British Lancaster and Halifax and
Stirling heavy bombers against the same industries of
Adolph Hitler, began.  The strikes were coordinated so that
the German workers and officials couldn't get started.  The
moment one bombed-out factory was re-built, it would

immediately be destroyed again. The minute they came back
to work after a night raid to try to build war planes or
ball bearings, workers would be blasted again from high
altitude in a daylight raid.

The Nazis didn't know whether they were coming or
going, whether to fart or go blind.

These strategic air operations were very
dangerous for crews from both the United States and Great
Britain. But soon the long-range bombing of industry began
to have a definite, if indirect, effect on actual
battlefield operations. The Germans began to learn that if
they didn't have supplies, fuel, ball bearings, equipment,
and rubber, they couldn't fight an effective war. With
devastating pin-point raids against the oil refineries at
Ploesti, Romania, and against the ball bearing factories at
Schweinfurt, and against the Focke-Wulf factories at Anklam
in Pomerania and many, many other strategic targets,
Germany was being badly hurt.

All of this blasting did, in July, 1943, become
"my" war. When I arrived in England, I was ready for it.

I was looking forward to it. I was afraid the
war was ending, and that if I didn't get into the air
quickly, I'd miss it.

But not until Uncle Sam sent me to flight school,

washed me out, and then sent me to my real calling, to teach me to be a high altitude precision strategic bombardier in a B-17 over Germany.

Only then did I learn the war was just getting started, and I was in it up to my ears.

## Chapter Three   Becoming a Bombardier

Uncle Sam didn't understand, probably didn't even have time to <u>care</u> that much, but my dream was to become a <u>pilot!</u>  At the beginning, that is. Busy old Sam had his hands full with what was happening in England as he put together one of the mightiest heavy precision bomber fleets the world had ever known. It was certainly immaterial to him that a young oil field worker in California wanted to help by fighting the war from the left hand seat of one of those bombers, or even the seat of a deadly quick fighter. I was very lucky, for gradually, as my "right foot start" antics in flight school commenced to catch up with me, I realized that I was <u>already</u> a damned good pilot. Hell, I was a pilot when I <u>went</u> to Air Corps flight school. I'd worked very hard to become a pilot in civilian life, and I had hundreds of hours in single engine and multi engine aircraft to prove it.

There was a problem with flight school, maybe because I was older than the other cadets.  I was more mature, they were still kids.  The rest of my flight school class responded well to what I considered to be bullshit, not that it did them much good, as you'll read later.  What happened to them was a damned shame. They were kids, yes, but a _good_ bunch of kids.

Sometimes, war _is_ hell.

To learn the military way to fly was the only reason I was at the Army Air Corps flight school at Santa Ana, California. Meanwhile, our group had no idea what was happening. The whole "airfield" was little more than a poorly groomed swamp. For ten days we sloshed around that mud flat in our civilian clothes, ruining our civilian shoes and generally deciding that the Army had its head up its ass. Apparently the brass hadn't caught up with us in those frantic early days. In fact, during my whole service career, the Army always seemed about ten days behind. Finally they pulled some of us out and sent us to Hemet, California, where we were to begin our flying training in the airplane affectionately known as the "Maytag Messerschmitt," the Ryan Trainer, the PT109, a harmless looking little two seater. All I wanted was to get on with it. I wanted to get to the war. I wanted no crap in the meantime, and no delays. Hell, somebody might kill Hitler and end the war while I was still fooling around with chicken-shit flight instructors and ancient little Ryans. I was ready to _go_!

Every pilot who has gone through it will tell

you, that isn't how it works.

But not understanding that fact was one of the luckiest things in my life, for it allowed me to become what every bomber pilot must secretly desire. It allowed me to become the single most important member of a highly trained combat crew. It allowed me to be the one to aim the bombsight and press the button, and accomplish what the whole thing was all about.

It allowed me to become a <u>bombardier</u>.

Let's get something straight about bombardiers. They say it never happened, but one American city <u>did</u> get bombed during the Second World War. It was the small town of Boyd City, Iowa, or Idaho, or something. They have a memorial plaque in town commemorating the unique event. The bombing happened in the middle of a dark night. One bomb exploded in the pleasant little square where the plaque is located, near the courthouse in the center of town. Another fell down the street, near the drug store, and another fell on down a little further, by the vet's office. Thank God, nobody was hurt and property damage was very light. There were some holes in the street, but little more. Still, bombs did fall on an American city during the Second World War.

They fell from an <u>American</u> bomber.

That's what I'd like to straighten out.

It's on the record.  A rookie bomber crew in training was on their way to a late-night practice mission over a bombing range hundreds of miles from the town.  I remember such night training missions in Blythe, California, where our crew dropped tons of bombs all over the desert, often not quite sure <u>what</u> we were blowing up.  This rookie crew spotted the lights from the town square, lights that looked remarkably like the lights around the target on the range, so the bombardier dropped his load.

To set the record positively straight, it was the rookie <u>navigator</u> who told the rookie bombardier that the range was below.  That's how it works.  The navigator gets you there, then you, the bombardier, take over.  It wasn't the bombardier's fault.  Bombardiers are usually the sharpest, smartest, best-trained member of any bomber crew, and often the best-looking and most macho, too.  In almost every case they have the best personality.  They can, and <u>do</u>, fly the airplane under the most harrowing circumstances, directly over the target, but the pilot, who normally flies the plane to and from the target, never drops the bombs. The pilot chauffeurs the plane to the area of the target, the bombardier, the most important member of the highly trained crew, takes over, flies directly to the target, then presses the button to complete the mission.

And to think that I once wanted to be a military pilot, and early on gave little consideration to becoming a precision bombardier. Well, you live and learn.

Flight school didn't, for me, last as long as for the others. Two things really turned me off. Not the drilling, the formations, the classes to attend, the hours and days of study, and certainly not the flying. I hadn't expected the life of a flight cadet in the Army Air Corps to be glamorous or easy. I knew it would be no bowl of cherries and that I would have to work very hard. I knew I could accept the necessary stuff. But the two unhappy circumstances combined to be the luckiest things of my service life till then. They got me in bombardier school, and they saved my life, in a roundabout way.

The first incident was when two upperclassmen crashed into our room at flight school while I was writing a letter home. Hell, it was late in the evening, after a long, hard day.

"Hit a <u>brace</u>!" they shouted at the top of their lungs, thoroughly enjoying themselves. Why they weren't in their own rooms studying or writing home I'll never know, but you could have heard them having their fun all the way into town.

My roomies jumped up and snapped to attention. Since I couldn't see any sense in such childish activity, I continued my letter.

"You!" they shouted at me, "Hit a brace right now!"

The second time didn't mean any more to me than the first. They were just young flight school students like me; younger than me, in fact, although further along in training. They probably didn't even have the solo hours in the air that I had, so I ignored them again. At that, both of them started to come at me in a threatening way. I put my pen down, folded my letter, and as my frightened roommates looked on, I threw both of the young jerks out of the room. Unfortunately for them, the door was just wide enough to accommodate one rushing human body, but not two, so they got their feathers ruffled a bit.

As I expected, the two cry-babies returned quickly with an officer who demanded an explanation for this apparently horrible breach of discipline.

"I'm here to fight a war, sir," I said calmly and with respect. "I have no time for this juvenile activity."

The officer, I believe, really understood and appreciated what I was saying, but again as I expected, there was some punishment to walk. I spent a few hours out on the ramp with a parachute strapped to my back, wasting valuable time marching back and forth, back and forth.

Of course the whole incident also went on my service record.

Foolish?  Yes.  I could have been studying, or flying.

Along with my class, I managed to complete the required 60 basic hours of Ryan trainer flying and we all went to Minter Field near Bakersfield, California.  We were to train in larger aircraft at Famosa, now a famous motor racing drag strip.  My record, of course, went with me, and was no doubt read in great detail by Lt. Lee Schrieber, a short, egotistical little prick who was to be my next instructor.  Each instructor at Minter had five students, and I was one of Lt. Schrieber's five.  The problem was, the other four were officers in grade going through pilot training.  I was the only cadet.  So Lt. Schrieber, the little bastard, would brief the others on the day's assignments over coffee and rolls in the officer's club.  Meanwhile, as a cadet, I would be standing formation or doing some other menial task.  I never knew what the hell was going on unless I happened to overhear one of the other instructors briefing their cadet students.

Life was not easy for Cadet Charlie Hudson,

especially since Lt. Schrieber, who otherwise appeared to despise his job, seemed to take great pleasure in showing me up and making me look bad in front of the four officer-students in our group. He would try to embarrass me and even ridicule me whenever possible. It got so bad that all I could think of was revenge. Lt. Schrieber's "instruction" was doing nothing to help me become a better pilot. Rather, his methods were filling my mind with ways to get even. One day my opportunity came, and it was the second major flight school incident that directed my life in a wonderful way.

Lt. Schrieber and I were in a trainer performing a low level pass for a landing. Suddenly he pulled back and caused the nose of the airplane to shoot straight up. Then he let go of the stick and said, "OK, Hudson, take it!"

That's when I decided to get my revenge on Lt. Schrieber.

Not that such a training tactic is bad. Flight instructors routinely set up situations that demand quick, correct action from students. If the student fails to take the right action, the flight instructor is there to sort things out. The time was coming for all of us when such a situation could occur and no instructor would be there to help. So, I understood what he was trying to do. I also knew what to do to bring the airplane back under control.

But this was Lt. Schrieber, the little son of a bitch who had been riding me constantly while he babied the other four in our group. I simply didn't respond at first, and as a very surprised Lt. Schrieber attempted to regain control of the airplane, I reached out and closed the throttle. Frankly, I hated the man so much that I was ready to kill us both. The engine dropped back to an idle, and very quickly the airplane began to fall, bucking and pitching back and forth. It then bounced wildly down the runway so hard I thought surely it would break its landing gear or even drop its wings. The plane was taking a terrible beating, and Lt. Schrieber was struggling, using all his skill to keep us from crashing. I think we plowed up three miles of cotton bushes until he finally regained control. He brought the plane around again and landed, never saying a word to me.

But after the airplane was parked, Lt. Schrieber began a verbal tirade that included every profanity I'd ever heard. He finally called me "the dumbest son of a bitch" he'd ever met. That really hurt my feelings. I may be dumb, but I'm no son of a bitch. It was, as oil field drillers used to say, "The length of pipe that broke the oil driller's back."

I climbed out of the airplane. As Lt. Schrieber was stepping down from the wing I reached out and grabbed him. In one single motion I hauled him the rest of the way down, spun him around, and leveled him with one of the best left jab, right cross combinations I'd thrown in many months. He went down hard and very quickly other students and instructors pulled me off before I could do further damage to the little jerk.

Needless to say, I spent the next few days restricted to my quarters under arrest, wasting more time while they set up my court-martial. That gave me time to think. I thought about my spotty career in the Army Air Corps. I thought about what they might do to me for slugging the little prick, an exercise I thought he richly deserved. I wondered if I could make it through flight school with guys like Schrieber in charge. <u>If</u>, that is, they <u>allowed</u> me to continue in flight school.

Did I really want this?

I thought about Mary, my beautiful dark-haired fiancée who was waiting at home in Taft, so near the base at Bakersfield.

"To <u>hell</u> with it!" I said to myself. They weren't really watching me, certain that I would never make

a break for it.  I called Mary and since she didn't know
all the details, she readily agreed to my romantic plan to
spend a few days in San Francisco.  We made an arrangement
to meet just outside the fence, and we were soon on our
way.  Not long after that, we were married, a marriage that
would last forty nine years.  I still can't conceive how
Mary managed to live with me so long, through the lonely,
frightening, trying times, and never knowing when she said
goodbye, as she did so often in our marriage, whether or
not she would ever see her husband again.  I finally lost
that sweet, loving woman to a heart attack in 1991, and I
still miss her very much.

For five days Mary and I made up for lost time
and I managed to put flight school and Lt. Schrieber and
the two-punch TKO out of my mind.  My friends were covering
for me.  Every night they took my bed out of the barracks
for bed check then replaced it before morning.  It didn't
appear that anybody was missing.  Lt. Schrieber was sure I
was enduring my restriction like a good cadet.

Returning to the barracks unnoticed, I was lying
on my bunk when two military policemen walked in.  My
civilian friends had interceded and persuaded Lt. Schrieber
to drop the charges against me.  But there was no way I
would be allowed to remain in flight school, not with my

record of insubordination.

You've seen the WW II movies about the poor young flight cadet who really wants to learn to fly, but who is all thumbs, or constantly in trouble, or who simply can't learn. He's already killed three instructors and two other students and frightened six control tower operators into retirement, and so the kindly squadron commander, an ace who has returned home from the war to teach young flyers, is finally forced to call him in. It is a difficult job, but somebody has to do it. The commander gently tells the young cadet that he's being washed out of flight school.

He's going to the front lines, or to bombardier school, whichever is worst.

What a crock of shit! They sent me to bombardier school back at Santa Ana, and it was the best thing that ever happened to me although I will admit that, at first, I felt I had disgraced myself and my family and my country by washing out. But at bombardier school I finally knew exactly what I wanted to be in the Air Corps. I put my whole heart and soul into bombardier training. Meanwhile, my original flight school class, a great bunch of guys, were upon graduation sent to Tampa, Florida, for training in the fast, twin-engined medium bomber, the B-26. I wound up my own military career in Tampa as a battle-scarred Lt.

Colonel in charge of several thousand men, but that was to
be three years later and not even in my wildest imagination
at the time.

You may have heard of the Tampa Bay Station in
those earlier war years. The place had a very unpleasant
reputation. In the Army Air Corps they used to say "one a
day in Tampa Bay." That wasn't supposed to be funny, but
the real meaning of the phrase was burned into me when I
learned that <u>every single one</u> of my classmates died in
training crashes in Tampa Bay. My right foot lead had
probably saved me again.

Santa Ana was a three month layover for future
bombardiers to learn advanced algebra, trigonometry,
calculus and other sciences I never knew existed. We were
also instructed in the workings of machine guns. If you
dropped your pencil in those bombardier classes at Santa
Ana, you could miss six weeks of instruction. It was fast
and furious. They needed trained bombardiers in Europe,
and we were it, and I for one was going to be ready.

It was impossible for me to believe, but probably
because I looked the toughest or could yell the loudest, or
maybe because I was the only cadet with GI issue gear, they
sewed a row of stripes to my sleeve and made me the Cadet
Colonel. Somehow they took a roughneck oil driller and

almost overnight turned him into an officer and a near-gentleman with an office and a staff in command of 20,000 troops for Sunday morning inspection drills and other functions.  Lt. Schrieber would have been proud.

Hell, I was proud.

Speaking of Lt. Schrieber, I did meet the little bastard again.  As a highly-decorated Major on a war bond selling tour, I had reason to be back at Minter three years later.  Waiting in the base exchange, I met several men I knew from before and we all had a happy, back-slapping, old-fashioned reunion.  We talked and laughed, and I told them the story about Lt. Schrieber and how I wound up as the lead bombardier for the entire Eighth Air Force in England. They broke up, informing me that Schrieber was still on the base. Somebody hurried to get him.  When he came in, he remembered me.  I sat there as a Major, my chest covered with battle stars and purple hearts and campaign ribbons and the French Croix de Guerre and other decorations, including my highly respected Distinguished Service Cross.

"I guess you've been doing pretty well," he mumbled, somewhat embarrassed.  He was still a Lieutenant.

Did I make it any easier for him?

Hell, no!

.

"Yeah, things took a turn for the better when I
left flight school," I answered with a chuckle. I still
didn't like the little prick and I never will.

Life continued to turn around for me at Williams
Field, our next stop as potential bombardiers. I was dead
serious by then as they introduced us to the most
sophisticated bombsight in the world, the Norden. This
bombsight, through manipulations by the bombardier, takes
into consideration several factors including air density,
wind force and direction, speed and position and drift of
the aircraft and other readings. Then it gradually centers
two crosshairs on a target that may still be miles ahead,
telling the bombardier, who is at that moment flying the
airplane into an exact position and attitude, precisely
when to drop the bombs. The Norden was a marvelous device.
I can remember seeing bombs dropping away to one side of
our airplane, all as a result of the calculations within
the bombsight. They hit the target squarely.

Only the planes of the commander and the deputy
commander on each bombing mission, I learned, had a Norden
bombsight. These two sights were quickly removed under
armed guard when those planes landed. The sights were
taken back to a sealed lab to be lubricated and cared for
and guarded. When the lead plane dropped, the other

bombardiers in the flight dropped.  If the lead plane was
shot down, or had to turn back, the second in command took
over and sighted on the target.  We were even told to shoot
our bombsights to death if it appeared we were going down,
but that, when it happened, only resulted in a bullet
bouncing around inside the airplane.  They were <u>tough</u>
little instruments.  Sure, the Germans had some of them
from shot-down B-17's and B-24's, but they had their own
precision bombing system so it wasn't really that big a
deal, after all.

Much later I would make modifications to my own
personal Norden, and would even build in "error" factors
when I was training newly-arrived bombardiers.  My work on
my own personal bombsight brought me in contact with our
bombsight officer, Don Million, and we were together so
much that we soon became personal friends.

Our group was sent to Kingman, Arizona, for three
weeks of live shooting at targets being towed by AT-6's.  I
guess those tow pilots were serving some kind of
punishment, or maybe they were some of Lt. Schrieber's
cadet students and he was busy with his officer students.
I remember thinking at the time how nice it would have been
if old Lt. Schrieber was flying one of the tow planes, and
I was on the guns.  By the time we got to Blythe,

California, we were forming into crews, and trying to work
together as a team. As a combat crew we went to Dyersburg,
Tennessee, where Mary joined me during my final training.
One month later, Mary and I said goodbye and I was sent to
Grand Island, Nebraska, for final staging. There we formed
our first air groups and received our combat flight gear
along with side arms and ammunition.

We were fighters at last, heading for the big
war.

My crew was issued its own private B-17 Flying
Fortress which, of course, we instantly loved. However,
because of its somewhat erratic and wobbly flying
characteristics, our new pilot named it "Punchy." Punchy
carried us to Gander Bay, Newfoundland, for refueling, then
across the Atlantic Ocean to Prestwick, Scotland.

There, Punchy was grounded and we were sent as a
crew to Bassingbourn, England, our new home for the next
couple of years. When we were assigned a new B-17, we
agreed to name it Punchy in honor of our first plane.

On Punchy's first combat mission, my right foot
starts hit again. Against my wishes, they assigned an
English observer to fly with the crew and point out
landmarks, coast lines, boundaries between countries,
potential targets and other identifying features. It

seemed to me that the bombardier needed to know these
things, to see what the enemy looked like, and should be
along on the flight, but the British observer required the
nose station usually occupied by the bombardier, so I
reluctantly stood down.  Over the English Channel the plane
directly below Punchy in the formation developed an
electrical fire in the cockpit, probably startling the
rookie pilot.  The plane suddenly and without warning
pulled straight up into the bottom of Punchy, and both B-
17's burst into flames and plunged into the cold water of
the Channel.  Rescue boats rushed in to help, but only a
few bodies were found.  Both crews were lost.  All of my
new friends were gone.  My first real wartime duty in
England was to report to the base morgue where, with heavy
heart, I endured the task of identifying the pals with whom
I'd trained.  I recognized our radio operator, Technical
Sergeant Paul Payne, and our pilot, Flight Officer W. C.
Edwards, and our navigator, Second Lt. D. B. Krist.  Also,
as the only officer left from the crew, I wrote letters to
the families of my friends, to try to share their
heartbreak with them.

       Deeply saddened at the loss of men I'd grown to
love, I had no crew and no airplane.  As a result I was
ordered to be a "fill in" bombardier on any other crew

needing my specialty.  I was not to be allowed the security
of flying with a crew I had come to know and trust.
Bewildered and lonely, I felt like a man without a country.

## Chapter Four   Exact Opposites, Missions One and Fifteen

A long distance bombing mission in heavy bombers
over enemy territory is a very dangerous, precisely
planned, carefully choreographed ballet of thousands of men
and many hundreds of bomber and fighter airplanes.  During
my combat days in B-17's I had no idea I would be
participating in other various and perhaps zany "precisely
planned" missions, including a famous airborne jailbreak
that could have been "choreographed" a little more
specifically, but one that still worked.  Or hauling
animals and snakes that broke loose in the airplane due to
heavy weather.  Or even having a contract out on my life,
and having to go into hiding for awhile, but all this did
happen, and more.  Earlier, though, my total concentration
was on bombing Adolph Hitler's factories and trains and
ships.

The quicker we smashed his war industry, the quicker the war would end. Sometimes a mission would work exactly as planned, sometimes it wouldn't. Flak might be far worse than expected, turning the mission. Or fighters might swarm up and drop B-17's like flies. Although flyers might joke about other flyers, there was never, to my knowledge, any serious attempt among the bomber crews who were flying missions to belittle German pilots, or pretend they were poor flyers. I recall a misguided company back home who came out with an advertisement showing a bomber pilot with a big grin on his face.

"Who's afraid of the new Focke-Wulf?" the smiling poster-pilot seemed to be demanding in big type across the colorful ad.

A B-17 Flying Fortress crewman with a sense of humor posted the ad on one overseas group's bulletin board, and then attached a piece of paper with a note that said "SIGN HERE." Every combat officer and enlisted man in the group signed the paper. The first signature was that of the Group Commander.

A heavy bombing mission involved intricate formations and complicated courses culminating over complex, difficult, and generally well-fortified enemy targets. It may not have appeared so in "Memphis Belle,"

with delays and indecisions and weather problems and fear
and young crewmen losing their virginity in the
bombardier's station and Army public relations people
hovering about (and these things did frequently occur,
except, perhaps, for the virginity matter), but everything
had to go exactly right for the mission to be a complete
success, for the target to be severely damaged or
destroyed, for many of the enemy to be killed.

Such missions were flown, in the height of the
battle, by B-17G's, the latest version of the bomber if you
don't count some following individual models with almost no
changes. The "G" had a chin turret with twin 50's below
the nose canopy. It was to be used, via a remote gun
sight, by the bombardier. Although specifications varied
greatly with altitude, air density, load, and even pilot,
most B-17G's had a service ceiling of nearly 36,000 feet.
Their maximum speed was in the 300 miles per hour range (at
30,000 feet) and they had a maximum continuous speed of
perhaps 270 miles per hour at around 25,000 feet.

That's in the book. In the field, they climbed
out at about 120 miles per hour, and they cruised at around
150 miles per hour, with a ceiling of around 25,000 feet.
Oddly, the paint on a B-17 could make a difference. If the
airplane was painted in camouflage colors during its

manufacture in the United States, its range was reduced
because of wind resistance to the somewhat less smooth
paint.  Later in the war, the camouflage "make-up" was
removed from most combat B-17's to increase speed and
range.            Although 12,731 B-17's were built in all the
series, beginning with the Boeing "299" and including the
"C," "D," "E," "F," and "G" models, counting 6,981 from
Boeing, 3,000 from Douglas and 2,750 from Lockheed, only a
few of these great airplanes are left in the world today.
A total of 4,750, carrying about 48,000 men, were lost on
actual combat missions, more than any other type of
aircraft.  Other B-17's flying at the end of the war went
into service for various countries as military and civilian
airplanes, even airliners, and most were eventually
scrapped or died of rust after being retired and parked at
some windswept, out-of-the-way landing field/airplane
graveyard. A few have been perfectly restored and preserved
in various air museums, including the famous "Shoo Shoo
Baby" B17G from Bassingbourn, now in the Air Force Museum
at Wright Patterson Air Force Base in Dayton, Ohio.  Shoo
Shoo Baby (now, in fact, with an extra "Shoo" on her nose
because some pilot liked it that way, thus making her Shoo
Shoo Shoo Baby), was found in a very deteriorated state and
was restored.  She is once again in a perfect state of

restoration and stands ready to fly at air shows.

Flying Fortresses, airplanes that did much of the fighting in the Second World War, shot down an average of twenty-three enemy planes on each thousand-plane raid, not to mention the massive and far more important damage they did on the ground. For the purpose of comparison, American fighters shot down an average of eleven fighters on the same raids.

The final model, the B-17G, had a maximum normal load of bombs between 2,600 and 8,000 pounds, depending on the type of bombs carried and other factors. Most G's carried up to thirteen Browning M-2 .50 caliber aircraft machine guns concentrated in six positions, including two each in three electrically powered turrets. This Flying Fortress had a maximum range of about 4,400 statute miles with a maximum fuel load of 3,569 Imperial gallons, or 3,300 miles with a normal fuel load of 2,490 Imperial gallons. There were about 180 Imperial gallons of oil aboard to lubricate the four mildly leaky Wright Cyclone, nine cylinder, air-cooled radial engines with Moss-General Electric turbo-superchargers. Engines ran at 2,300 revolutions per minute and developed about 1,200 horsepower at takeoff. Each engine had a three paddle-bladed Hamilton Standard propeller with a five foot, 9 1/2 inch radius, and cowl flaps that opened and closed to regulate cylinder head temperature.

Often the reliable Wright-Cyclone engines continued to function with some cylinders damaged by flak.

The wings of a G spanned 109 feet, 9 inches. The airplane was 74 feet, 4 inches long and 19 feet, 1 inch high. It weighed slightly over 36,000 pounds empty.

A "Squadron" of B-17's was made up of from 6 (at the beginning of the war) to 18 airplanes (at the height of the battle). A "Group" included four Squadrons, although only three squadrons generally flew at any one time, with the fourth standing down for a day of rest and recuperation. In a "Wing" were five Groups. Three Wings made up a "Division," and three Divisions made up the Eighth Air Force all across England. When the entire Eighth Air Force flew on a bombing mission, there were formations more than 150 miles long over England, a country only 100 miles wide in places. There were, when the Eighth Air Force flew, nearly two thousand B-17 Flying Fortresses in the sky at one time, and many hundreds of fighter planes to protect them, all heading for an unfortunate but generally well-defended target in Europe. There were nearly twenty one thousand men in the sky, including the fighter pilots.

Who would ever have thought at the beginning that
right-foot-starting Second Lieutenant Charlie Hudson would
eventually become Lt. Col. Charles S. "Combat" Hudson, and
fly several times as lead Eighth Air Force bombardier with
a full General as pilot, and in a sense have an entire Air
Force drop when he dropped?

Who would ever have thought that those precise
bomber formations would also be "used" in other strange
ways, including the "purple heart corner" of the formation?
The lowest and last position in a flight of bombers could
be used to play a dirty trick on an incoming officer of
rank.  Until, that is, they figured out what was happening,
or died trying.  Each squadron's "TO," or Table of
Organization, allotted so many ranks; so many Captains, so
many Majors, and so on.  Since these figures were often
calculated back in the United States by desk-bound officers
far from the battle, they didn't generally change.

Let's say we had a very well-liked Captain who
was finishing his missions and getting ready to go home.
Because he was a popular guy, the squadron hoped to promote
him and send him back to the United States as a Major.
He'd get a better military job with more responsibility,
his wife and kids would be proud, and it would be a great
thing for his income, too.

The trouble could be, the new officer coming in as a replacement may already be a Major. So there would go the promotion of the well-liked Captain because the squadron wasn't authorized another Major on it's TO.

There was, however, a possible solution to this dilemma. What would happen, for example, if the new man didn't last very long in the squadron? What would happen if his luck was bad and he got shot down on his first or second mission? That would mean a slot for a Major would re-open in the squadron, and a Captain could be promoted.

Harsh? Consider it this way. The new guy may be a real peach, a splendid fellow, but nobody knew him yet. Somebody had to fly in purple heart corner. Why should it be somebody very popular, somebody who had flown their share of missions, who may have begun in that dangerous part of the formation? Why should it be a crew near to going home? The new major just naturally got the assignment. If luck was with him, and he lasted long enough, he could eventually fly in a more protected place in the formation, be well-loved by the troops, and maybe even complete his missions and go home with a promotion to Lt. Colonel. Providing, that is, his replacement wasn't already a Lt. Colonel, in which case the even newer officer would get the rear position.

Meanwhile, if the incoming Major should .
immediately get shot down from purple heart corner, all we
could hope for was that he survived, as many did, and made
it to some German prisoner of war camp.  Meanwhile we would
have an opening to promote our rotating Captain to Major.

Like I said, war is hell, and we all had to take
our chances.

A combat mission sometimes didn't go as planned.
For example, as the fill-in bombardier at Bassingbourn
after the loss of Punchy, I was briefed <u>nine times</u>, for
nine different missions on nine different crews, before
everything, including the weather, came together and we
actually took off on my first combat bombing mission over
enemy territory.

This finally occurred on September 23, 1943, and
by the time we actually headed for Europe, I was <u>ready</u>!  I
didn't much care <u>whose</u> airplane I was in, just so we headed
for an enemy target.

Here's how a mission was supposed to work.

Each B-17 Flying Fortress crew was made up of
commissioned officers and enlisted men, a total of ten men
on a regular crew.  The pilot, co-pilot, navigator and
bombardier were commissioned officers.  The pilot was in
command, the co-pilot was the executive officer. The flight

engineer (who was also the top turret gunner), radio
operator/gunner and other assigned gunners (two waist
gunners, a tail gunner, and a belly turret gunner) were
enlisted men, usually sergeants or higher. Of course the
bombardier, a commissioned officer with extra training who
worked in the nose, also became a nose gunner, or a "chin"
gunner in the latest B-17G's, before and after the bomb
run. The navigator plotted the course and also operated
"cheek" guns, sticking out the side of the lower front
compartment. Everybody but the pilot and co-pilot fought,
and the co-pilot had to be there in the right hand seat to
fly the airplane in case the pilot was killed or injured,
which, although they were somewhat protected by armor
plating front and rear, did happen.

Officers and enlisted men slept in different
quarters, so, hours before dawn, people went to enlisted
men's barracks and officer's rooms to awaken those
scheduled to fly on a mission that day. Many hours before
that, in command centers far away, the decisions had been
made by Generals about which target to hit, and when to hit
it. Orders had been chattering down on teletype machines
to various Group headquarters throughout England, then to
Squadrons. Crews dressed in their electric underwear and
bulky flight gear collected their equipment and weapons,

then, still half asleep in the wee hours of the morning,
headed for breakfast.  After that, on a strict time
schedule, they met in briefing rooms.  On the front walls
were great maps of Europe with recently stretched strings
or red crayon lines indicating courses emanating from
Bassingbourn and the other bases involved, maps that often
drew groans from those in attendance, depending upon the
obviously marked targets.

   In the briefing room, crews heard from various
section heads with information from various departments.
Fighting to stay awake, crews listened to the latest
intelligence about the target, the strength of the
protective escort of fighters, the rendezvous point with
other groups of airplanes, the opposition expected, and the
all-important weather.  After the station time
announcement, that time when crews were to report to their
planes, all wrist watches were synchronized to the watch of
the group navigator who, presumably, had synchronized his
watch to some greater master time.

   Outside, from widely scattered pads where the
great B-17's had been parked to prevent destroying a whole
group of them with one enemy bomb, the whining sound of
starting engines drifted all the way to the briefing room.
Ground crews were doing their final work, getting the

airplanes ready to fly and fight.

    After briefing, some of the crews reported to the Chaplain, who was sleepily waiting in another room in the building to hear confessions or to offer encouragement. With nothing else to fill my time in those cold, damp, pre-dawn English hours before station time, I sometimes went to that room to visit that man myself. Hell, it couldn't hurt.

    A combat philosophy of mine having nothing to do with religion, and one which may not have worked for others, was right for me.  Of course, I never discussed it with my lovely wife, Mary.  I'm not a pessimist, nor do I, fortunately, put faith in that ideology that says, "What you think is going to happen, is going to happen." Everybody handles combat in his own way.  Deep down in my heart, I convinced myself to believe I would not return from any bombing mission over enemy territory.  Pretty damned sure that we would be shot down, or at least that I would be killed, I lived the night before in London as though it were my last night.  Sometimes I literally staggered into the briefing room.  But what the hell, I wasn't coming back from the mission, so I wanted to go out in a blaze of glory.  It was generally quite a surprise to me to see Bassingbourn in the distance after a mission, for I was sure I would never see home again.  Even then I

wasn't certain we would land safely, shot up as we often
were.

Before they left the briefing area, airmen always
picked up "box lunches" from the bombardier of each crew.
I don't know why the bombardier passed them out, but that's
how it was, and it was our job to collect them back if the
mission was scrubbed.  We were to chew out any man who
didn't return his box lunch if the mission was aborted, but
we usually didn't get them back.  Nor did we usually chew,
either. The lunches consisted mostly of chocolate candy
bars and other quick-energy confections.  The boxes were
accepted with a grin, because everybody knew that most of
the candy would end up with London's chocolate-starved
sweethearts, instead of being eaten on the upcoming
mission, or handed back to the bombardier.  I remember one
mission over Dessau when we were getting hit hard with
flak.  I had my eye on the sight but I was getting bounced
back and forth so aiming was very difficult.  Just then a
voice came over the intercom from one of the gunners.

"Is it OK if I eat my candy bar now, Major
Hudson?"

This did break the extreme tension of a difficult
moment.

Meanwhile, what each crewman brought to the

Fortress was what they had; coffee in thermos jugs, water, or other food.  There were no toilets on most Flying Fortresses, but a few had a firmly attached white can in the rear before the tail gunner's position, a very public can that could be used in an emergency and perhaps from which the slang term "can" derives.  Every bomber also had a "pilot's relief tube" that could be used by the crew, a tube that sprayed urine on the enemy - though he probably didn't notice.  The relief tube led out through the bottom of the Fort to a discharge nipple.  Inside, the tube had a movable funnel-shaped end that hooked to the bulkhead when not in use, and that could be unhooked and held at an appropriate height when in use.  Brand-new rookie radio operators were sometimes told by the Fort's flight engineer that the funnel-shaped device was a special airplane inter-com, to be used by pressing the funnel closely to the face and shouting loudly in an effort to communicate.  All of this hazing was done to the delight of the more veteran crew members.

Reporting to the airplane before dawn, crews readied stations, machine guns and other items.  Bombs and bullets had already been loaded by ground crews, and top secret bombsights had been brought under armed guard to the two lead ships.  Navigators pored over maps under their little compartment map lights, pilots and co-pilots walked around the dark, menacing bombers with flashlights looking for last minute hydraulic leaks or other problems. Lead bombardiers crawled into nose compartments to check bombsights and targets and forward guns, and radio operators warmed up equipment by talking to ground stations. Gunners very carefully checked their shining clean weapons.

Then perhaps began a period of waiting...and waiting...and _more_ waiting. Often the first signs of daylight streaked the sky to the east, over Europe, as the waiting continued. Crews sat around talking...or dozing...or praying, depending upon whether the upcoming mission, if it flew at all, was considered to be a "milk run" or a very hazardous assignment from which many of the great bombers would almost certainly not return.

Because I had been scrubbed so often, I wore my pajamas under my flight gear, a fact that became known to the media, and about which they made a big point. Some of my missions were accomplished in pajamas, and on the missions where I was wounded, the doctors at the base hospital would chuckle when they cut my flight gear away from my body and found night clothes.

Sometimes the entire mission was scrubbed and

hundreds or even thousands of crews waiting across England would merely go back to bed, which is why I wore pajamas. Maybe the weather closed in at the target, or over the channel, or maybe the opposition wasn't calculated correctly.  Or maybe the target had been reevaluated.

But if the mission was ordered to proceed, heavy-laden bombers lined up in long, closely knit, nose to tail, stop-and-go rows, jerking and lumbering ponderously forward along taxi strips with brakes squealing as they moved slowly toward their turn at the end of the runway.  Then, ordered by flares fired from the control tower every thirty seconds, they roared off from many different bases, one by one into the dawn, breaking out of the cloud cover at perhaps 10.000 feet.  There, very carefully, the huge airplanes began an almost impossibly complex, dance-like procedure of assembling into combat formations.  Sometimes for two hours the lead planes would circle in the breaking dawn, firing off rockets of various colors to identify them to their own wing aircraft.  On the ground, a "buncher" beamed a radio signal to be used by the enlarging formation as the Flying Fortresses continued a vast 360 degree circle over England, each formation from each base joining other formations in the precise ballet needed to form the American armada.  Finally, as the magnificent group turned

on a heading for their unlucky target in Europe, the sky
seemed filled with thundering B-17 Flying Fortresses. All
around, for as far as the eye could see, was a vast fleet
of heavy bombers, layer upon layer of them, each manned
with a fighting crew ready for battle. As the first planes
reached Europe, the ones in the rear of the formation might
still be over England.

      I never tired of watching from my bombardier's
picture window the precision, the raw beauty of mighty
machines of death and destruction thundering to their
victim, of feeling the inestimable power all across the
sky.
When it was still dark, the four dots of fire from the
engine of each exhaust of nearby Forts could be seen,
hundreds of dots of fire in the darkness, as the group
roared toward Europe. Then, at dawn, with the sky
lightening to grey, mighty Flying Fortresses were visible
all around, each maintaining its own precise position in
the array of protective formations, each one watching out
not only for itself, but for its companion wing airplanes.
Most airmen felt it was one of the most awe-inspiring
sights imaginable.

      The precision was necessary. Once, after a
bombing run, a confused and lonely B-17, battered and

staggering, attached itself to the wrong group of
airplanes. It was a group that was pre-planned to fly to a
base in Africa.  Sadly, the stray B-17 didn't have nearly
enough fuel to make the long journey, and finally it
ditched into the Mediterranean Sea, where it rests today.

Along with its crew.

As the great band of bombers headed for the
target, pilots began their standard warning to crews.  The
B-17 is non-pressurized, and except for the front end, non-
heated, so hundreds of pilots spoke over hundreds of
intercoms.

"It's forty below outside, guys, and we're now at
twenty-two thousand feet.  Keep your eyes peeled for enemy
fighters.  Wear your oxygen masks at all times, put on your
flak jackets, and hook up your safety straps."  The order
about safety straps on parachute harnesses was given in
case a plane suffered a direct hit, in the hope that the
extra strap might prevent a crewman from falling out.  In
fact, it did on my third mission, as you will read.  "If
you must move around," pilots continued, "use a walkaround
bottle.  And don't touch your guns with your bare hands,"
the pilot always reminded.  "You'll freeze to them."
Finally the order to test guns was given, and all around
the sky, from each heavy machine gun in each bomber, a

burst of bullets was fired.

It must have resembled a heavy shower of rain on the water far below as the thousands of bullets all hit together.

With everything nearly ready, smaller fighter escorts began to skim in at pre-determined coordinates, joining the mighty armada of bombers. A wonderfully warm and welcome sight to the bomber crews, the fighters eased into their own battle formations overhead, ready to pounce on enemy fighters who might attempt to sneak in and hurt the majestic bombers below. The entire vast, complicated mission proceeded to the target. By this time, adrenalin was pumping in every crewman.

Who would live through the day, and who would die?

Who would make it home, and who would plunge to the ground trapped in a spinning, falling, burning bomber?

Who would enjoy dinner that night with friends, and who would eat slop in a German prisoner of war camp?

Combat was near, and every eye was on the brightening sky around, searching for enemy fighters, waiting for the inevitable enemy flak from anti-aircraft batteries on the ground, ready and willing to fight to the death. Winston Churchill said something else, and he was right.  "There is no greater thrill for a man than to be shot at in anger," said England's Prime Minister, "and missed."

Only the eyes of the bombardier on each plane were not directed outward.  The closer the fleet drew to the target, the busier he became.  He had to crawl back and "arm" the bombs by removing safety rings from the nose of each one, rings he would hand in at the end of the mission if all went well.  He was also busy adding last minute corrections and calculations on drift and air temperature and density and other matters into the bombsight, preparing for the bombing run when he would take control and fly the airplane as he centered the crosshairs on the target far below and ahead.

After nine scrubs, my tenth briefing was for a mission over Nantes, up an inlet on the western shore of France.  If I had possessed the ability to look into the future, and to see my second, third and fourth missions, and several others, I might not have been so anxious to get started on my first.  But I _was_ anxious.  The target was a row of concrete-reinforced submarine pens and a U-boat supply ship, in port for re-loading.  If we could damage the pens severely enough, German subs at sea would have no place to make port.  If we could sink the supply ship, a

number of U-boats at sea, boats killing our convoys, would
run out of fuel and torpedoes and food, and the Nazi crews
would do without their mail from home, and many German
submarines would be forced to turn and slink to some port,
somewhere, or die at sea.  Maybe one of our troop ships
would survive if we hit our targets directly, and thousands
of our soldiers would live for awhile longer, perhaps even
eventually to come home to loved ones.

As a brand-new, wet-behind-the-ears shavetail
Second Lieutenant bombardier still awaiting assignment to a
permanent crew, I was ordered into the nose station of a
sleek B-17 by the name of "Eagle's Wrath."  Waiting there
in the dark, <u>wanting</u> to go, <u>anxious</u> to drop my bombs on the
sub nest and the mother ship, I thought about what every
other bombardier in the Air Corps sooner or later
considered.

Far in the future, a television show by the name
of "M*A*S*H," a show about a different war but with the
same death and destruction, would cover the topic in
emotional detail.  In a sad and moving story, it would tell
of a young American B-29 bombardier who would suddenly turn
himself off, phase himself out, who would be brought into
the MASH forward hospital quietly and firmly convinced that
he was Jesus Christ returned.  Not <u>meant</u> to be funny, it

would not _be_ funny, but it would be moving and absorbing.
The young bombardier would not answer to his own name, or
acknowledge that he was anybody but Jesus.  He would have
intelligent conversations with MASH character Lieutenant
Frances Mulcahey, a Catholic priest.  The confused young
bombardier would even partially convince another beloved
MASH character, company clerk "Radar" O'Reilly, that he was
indeed who he said he was.  He would be led by young Radar
to a spot behind a tent and there, in an intensely moving
scene, shyly but sincerely asked to lay hands upon and
"bless" Radar's teddy bear.  Finally, in a following scene
that brought tears to the eyes of combat veterans who faced
death at every turn, he would bless Radar, himself, though
he would call him by his given name of "Walter."  Even
wise-cracking doctor Hawkeye Pierce would refuse to make
fun of the young bombardier who had become Jesus Christ as
a result of the unimaginable pressure of his job, allowing
the likable young man to keep his strong belief.  Only
Major Frank Burns, at whom every other MASH character poked
fun, ridiculed the unique patient, who Burns said was a
coward trying to avoid further combat.  The confused
bombardier, overwhelmed by a job that sometimes included
random death and destruction of innocent women and
children, would finally leave the front line hospital for

stateside psychiatric treatment, still believing with all
his heart that he was Jesus Christ.

How <u>does</u> it feel to drop high explosives on
relatively innocent people, maybe factory or dock workers
who are only trying to earn a living, maybe even women and
children, with the inevitable near misses?  How <u>do</u> you
handle it?  That is, if it "feels" like anything at all, or
needs "handling?"

It didn't matter one bit to me, so I didn't have
to "handle" anything.  I didn't have an identity complex.
I knew exactly who I was and what I was doing.  I was
Charlie Hudson, an officer and a bombardier in the Army Air
Corps. It was my duty.  It was what my country trained me
for.  We didn't ask for the war, Adolph Hitler did.  If his
German people wanted to follow him, that was their choice.
So I didn't spend any time at all thinking about such
things, except to know that every bomb I released could
measurably shorten the war, and save the lives of American
soldiers on the ground, men I frankly considered to be far
more important and valuable than any German, citizen or
soldier, man, woman or child.

In other words, everybody on the ground was the
enemy.  If I still had bombs, and there was a German city
below, it didn't make any difference at all to me that they

might be innocent when I dropped.  They were Germans, so
they were the enemy.

We finally roared off the Bassingbourn runway
into the grey eastern dawn on my first mission in Eagle's
Wrath, heading for France.  Because my crew had been lost
in the crash of Punchy, I was an extra, and filled in where
needed. Years later, one of my regular pilots and a
personal friend, Bud Evers, said, "It was tough on Charlie
because he didn't have a regular crew to become familiar
with, to become close to.  He was shuffled from crew to
crew and then when he became the lead bombardier he flew
with the general in whatever plane led the mission.  His
job was more difficult because of all of this."

Our pilot on my first mission was Lt. Bill
Jewett, about whom you will hear more in a moment.  Inside
my nose bubble, I probably got the best view of all.  I
looked to the east.  On my way at last with a full bomb
load and guns ready, I felt confident.  I felt good.  There
was no fear.  Well-trained to know what to do, I looked
forward to the coming battle with great anticipation.  I
wasn't coming home anyhow, so I might as well get the most
from it.  I was already a dead man, and dead men feel no
fear.

Not until I began to consider the alternatives,

that is, when the fighters attack and the flak rips into
the airplane and you suddenly discover that you might <u>not</u>
die cleanly, on the spot, with no memory at all of the
chunk of steel that killed you.  Instead, you might be
horribly injured, or cooked in a fire, and then be forced
to live on. You might be blown out of the airplane and fall
to the ground with a useless parachute, or no parachute at
all.  You might lose an arm or a leg, or your sight, but
not your life.

      <u>Damn</u>! You might even get your <u>balls</u> shot off.

      <u>Then</u> I began to feel some fear.

      But we were on our way to France, and from the
nose of the B-17 Eagle's Wrath, from my own point of view,
it seemed to be on the way to a real disappointment.  Where
was the curtain of flak we'd been briefed about?  Where
were the darting, dangerous young German fighter pilots
from Hitler's famous Luftwaffe?

      Where was the <u>action</u>?

      We droned along over the cold, choppy North Sea
nearly four miles below, eyes peeled for trouble.  In my
journal for that mission, I wrote, "I was leaning out of
the nose of the airplane, eagerly seeking my first look at
flak."  I had for weeks been living among fighting men, men
who were accustomed to being shot at from the ground, and

who were battling fighter planes in the air every day.
Their casual conversation at meals and other gatherings had
convinced me that combat over Europe was real, where men
are men.  Now here we were flying along unmolested and with
the target in sight in the distance.

      I was rather disappointed with the calm
tranquility of my very first combat bombing mission.  It
wasn't at all as I had expected.

      Until one thunderous, intense instant later, when
a sudden burst of flak over the nose of Eagle's Wrath tore
into my compartment with a fury that was totally unexpected
and with a force far beyond anything I had imagined.  Glass
from the upper nose blister and windows smashed down on me,
hurling me to the floor of the compartment like a rag doll.
Lying in a heap, I carefully felt my face to see if I was
alive, if I was bleeding.  But before I could inspect my
gloves, enemy fighters and friendly fighters streaked into
view far overhead, above the flak.  Meanwhile, the flak
continued with intense concentration all around us.  German
gunners on the ground had calculated our altitude
perfectly, and anti-aircraft shell bursts shook our B-17
one way and then another, ripping into her wings and
fuselage with jagged chunks of steel.  Several of the Forts
around us trailed smoke from one or more damaged engines,

though each one seemed able to continue the mission.

From somewhere overhead, falling down in front of us, a German fighter plane twisted slowly in flames. I saw no parachute open for the Luftwaffe pilot. Not only was this real combat to a brand-new bombardier, but later, back at the base, I heard several experienced flyers comment that it was some of the worst, and most accurate flak they had encountered. Apparently the Nazis were very anxious to protect the sub supply ship far below. We could see flashes in groups of four from the ground. These were from clusters of four anti-aircraft batteries. Then, less than a minute later, we would see four flashes of fire and black smoke appearing in the sky in front of our formation, or slightly to one side or the other. They had us in their crosshairs.

I watched the lead bomber carefully, my own bomb bay doors open and my finger on the bomb toggle switch of our ship. When he dropped his bombs, I dropped mine, then I jumped quickly back to the twin fifties in the nose. Just in time, in fact, to fire about thirty rounds into the belly of a Focke Wulf streaking past above.

For some reason, the lead B-17 turned west and headed out to sea rather than turning east and heading home over France. Ours was not to reason why, ours was to

follow the lead ship and so, do-or-die and full of flak
holes, we followed.  Soon we lost our escort of both
friendly and enemy fighters.  They may have wondered why we
were heading out to sea, but with their fuel supplies low,
they headed back to their respective friendly or enemy
airfields.

Droning on, we watched the Atlantic below and the
sky all around.  Slowly we turned to a new course that
would lead us up the English Channel toward Bassingbourn.
The formation by then was well scattered, with a number of
smoking stragglers far below and behind.  Battered Eagle's
Wrath was doing well enough.  As we came into the Channel,
a small band of Focke Wulfs jumped the group in front of
us, ignoring us and the other easy-prey stragglers below
and behind.  Perhaps they didn't see us, scattered as we
were.  When one of the Germans plummeted into the water
below, the others turned and headed for home.

So did we.  Very low on fuel, a last minute
decision was made to land with damaged wheels down rather
than attempting a belly-landing with the wheels up.  Our
pilot, Lt. Jewett, made the decision and I agreed, having
seen several belly landings at Bassingbourn that quickly
turned to worms with explosions after the plane stopped
skidding.  I even mentioned at the time that I would prefer

to bail out than to belly land, although later in my combat
career I would have chosen to stay with the plane under
similar circumstances.

Mission number one ended with a rough, bouncing
landing, and the ice had been broken for Lt. Charles S.
"Combat" Hudson. With pleasure and a new sense of
confidence I spoke of the mission to others that night at
dinner. I was no longer a virgin. I had faced the enemy,
and prevailed. That inner fear of being shot down on my
first mission, before ever dropping a bomb, was gone. I'd
made it.

By the end of my Air Corps career, although I had
no idea then, I would be lead bombardier of the entire
Eighth Air Force. I would be battered and scarred and
decorated, and wiser, but always proud of what I was doing
to help win the war.

Years later one of my employees at a golf course
was looking through some of my notes about that first
mission, and about Lt. Jewett. She was amazed because Lt.
Jewett, who simply told his Commanding Officer that he
would never again fly a mission into Germany, was her
father. He was a good man and a good pilot. He was no
coward, but he simply was not cut out for combat flying and
he knew it, and so did his CO. Lt. Jewett was assigned

duties in England as Operations Officer for another squadron. I'm told he served well, and that is perhaps as it should have been.

I was also told by a reliable source that in the next six weeks after that mission, the first one for me, Bill Jewett's hair turned snow white. His daughter confirmed this.

Regrets? Sure. I regretted missions like number fifteen on April 27, 1944, to Cherbourg, to blast some secret German gun emplacements. By then I was a Captain in the 91st Bombardment Group, and had been awarded several Air Medals, a Distinguished Flying Cross, and my DSC, as well as more than one Purple Heart. I was an old-timer. The flak was monstrous that day over France. It was bursting all around us, cutting us to ribbons. One chunk of shrapnel ripped up through the map I was studying as we approached the target, another hit our navigator, Captain William Borellis, in the back, puncturing his flak suit and lodging in his parachute harness, but not injuring him.

Number four engine burst into flames but our pilot, Lt. Bob Roberts, feathered it and the fire blew out. Ahead, a B-17 took a direct hit and dove straight into the ground. I saw no parachutes floating behind.

My roommate, Jim O'Looney, was on that ship.

Later, I did get a card from Jim, forwarded through the Red Cross. He was in a prisoner of war camp in Germany, and was telling me that I could have the clothing and booze he'd left behind in the room. Hell, I was wearing his clothes that day, and the booze was gone before he hit the ground.

Meanwhile, the flak over Cherbourg was devastating, driving us from the target. Our group was finally forced to turn sharply away and head for the coast, but the intense flak began again over the Guernsey Islands. We were on three engines, dropping further and further behind the formation, and had no hope of doing any damage at all. I dropped our bombs into the water, for the first time becoming a distasteful "chandelier," then sat and sweated as the formation, with every ship full of holes, headed for home. Many men were killed and many others wounded that day and we had bombed only the English Channel. We had killed no Germans, blasted no secret gun emplacements, and done nothing at all to shorten the war.

I hated it, but it couldn't be helped.

Sometimes missions didn't work as they should.

## Chapter Five    Missions Two and Three

The reason my picture appeared in publications
across the United States carrying the "Strange As It Seems"
feature back in 1944 was not necessarily because I was

"strange," though some might argue the point.  It was, according to the author of that popular newspaper column, because I was decorated for being in the thick of it, and for having at least something to do with men coming back alive who might otherwise have not, on three of my first four WW II B-17 combat missions over Europe.  Call it luck, call it bravery, call it a hatred of seeing a comrade die, call it adrenalin, call it patriotism, call it whatever you wish, but three of my first four missions were absorbing for the entire crew, especially the bombardier.  Some B-17 Flying Fortresses made it through the whole war without a scratch, my Fortresses seemed to attract the enemy.  You've read about mission number four in the first chapter of this book, and number one as well.  Consider two and three in a moment.

They were each a real barn-burner for the entire crew.

First, though, a word about mission number nineteen, just to show that everything didn't always blow up in Charlie Hudson's face.  It was an early morning flight on May 9, 1944, to bomb a German airfield at St. Dizier, France, about a hundred miles east of Paris.

The final outcome of a combat mission could never be accurately predicted.  Some missions were very rough;

they were missions where we got shot up but still hit the target. On other missions we missed the target but still got shot full of holes and had casualties. Or, maybe we would <u>not</u> get shot up, but because of weather or for some other reason, miss the target. Rarely did we enjoy a mission like number nineteen to blow up the airstrip in France, especially since by then everything we did pointed directly to the massive ground invasion of Europe we all knew was coming. Destroying a landing strip in France as we were scheduled to do almost certainly had a connection with the invasion. Our action would, if successful, help prevent German war planes from taking off to bomb or strafe Allied soldiers and marines on an invasion beach somewhere. We didn't know "D Day" would be on June 6, 1944, with hundreds of thousands of Allied troops storming the bloody shores of France at Normandy, but we knew it couldn't be too far in the future or too far from where we were bombing.

The pilot on mission number nineteen was my best friend, Captain John Davis; the co-pilot was Wing Leader Colonel Ross Milton.

We were to be the lead plane of the formation, making me the lead bombardier. Every other bombardier would be watching my B-17, and would release their bombs when I released mine. I was the one with the bombsight, as usual. The morning was crisp and cool when we boarded our Fortress. Dawn was just breaking. It was a beautiful, calm morning, with a clean, moist, English feel to the air of Bassingbourn. We all felt as good as possible under the circumstances. It was one of those mornings when you felt pretty sure the day was going to work out well. I had trouble convincing myself that I wasn't going to return from the mission. Men and women who flew in the war will know what I mean when I say that even the airplane smelled especially nice that morning.

Combat veterans who've been there will remember the smell of the inside of a ready-to-fight military airplane, bomber or fighter. It isn't a bad smell at all, but rather a very specific combination of fuel and oil and electricity and gunpowder and metal and other more subtle aromas of canvas and GI issue clothing and equipment. Once you smell it, you never forget it. Let's say you attend a local air show decades later, and on the ramp is an old bomber or fighter from World War II. Even though it may have been completely torn down and restored with many new and rebuilt parts after sitting unattended on some windswept field in the desert for years, the same aroma is still apparent when you crawl aboard. It never goes away.

Olney 104

A civilian might not even notice it, but it can bring tears
to the eyes of a former military flyer, and flyers know it.
It didn't bring tears to my eyes, not on that crisp
Bassingbourn morning, but the smell of a combat-ready B-17
seemed especially nice all the same.

        The flight to St. Dizier was calm and uneventful.
When coastal flak opened up on a flight in front of us, we
merely changed our heading slightly and watched it off to
one side.  Very soon in the distance ahead on that bright,
clear morning, the French airfield we were to bomb became
distinct.  With the bomber under my control, 1 cranked last
minute corrections into the bombsight and waited for the
exact instant to release the bombs.  Everything was
perfect, every factor was in synchronization.  The target
crept nearer the crosshairs in the bombsight.  For just a
moment the auto-pilot malfunctioned and the plane began to
climb, but John Davis quickly brought it back on course.  I
waited...waited...then, exactly on target, I released the
bombs.  Never in my experience as a bombardier did I hit a
target more squarely than I did that day at St. Dizier.
Every other bombardier in the fleet dropped when I dropped,
and we plastered the airfield and buildings with delayed
action bombs.  Later they began to blow up and the target
was blown completely apart.  The German-held airfield was

mauled, it was blown away, it was in a few blinding minutes
rendered totally useless to the Nazis.  Obviously it would
take years to re-build before it could be ready to fight
off an invasion.  The Germans, we knew, didn't have years.

As we headed back toward the coast from St.
Dizier  following another bomber group who had hit a target
nearby, I noticed on my map that if we continued on the
current heading we would fly directly over the big airfield
at Romilly.  The last time we did that, the flak was so
heavy that many of our planes didn't make it home.

I informed Captain Bill Borellis, our navigator,
and he called pilot John Davis.  Davis, in turn, quickly
radioed the lead group and told them that according to
Charlie Hudson, they were flying directly into a very
dangerous flak area.  But the word came back from Col. Jim
Berry that their navigator disagreed, and that they didn't
plan to change course.  Borellis, who got the word from
Davis, told me.

Re-checking my map, I said, "If we don't change
course quickly, we're going to get hit <u>hard</u>!"  Borellis
told Davis, then added, "If Charlie says you should turn,
then <u>turn</u>.  He can <u>smell</u> flak!"

"OK, OK," said Davis, turning our plane and our
entire group of planes to what I recommended, ten degrees

to the right. Along with some other bombardiers, I'd taken
the time to train and become certified as a "DR" navigator,
an expert in dead reckoning, and I was certain I was right.

Ahead, guns on the ground around Romilly suddenly
opened fire, and the other flight began to take direct
hits. In less than three minutes, three B-17's and crews
went down in flames. Not one of our planes took a single
hit.

For us, it had been a successful mission. We
lost no airplanes, and had no wounded over whom to fire
flares on our final approach to alert the waiting
ambulances on the ground. As we rolled down the runway at
Bassingbourn, I knew that it had been a perfectly executed,
completely successful bombing mission. It was sad to see
some of our comrades go down from the lead flight, but we
had done our best to warn them.

Later that night at dinner, Berry argued with
John Davis.

"Why didn't you _insist_?" Berry demanded. "Why
didn't you put some _pressure_ on to get me to turn away?"

Davis could only look at him sadly. "We _did_ tell
you to turn, Colonel," he answered calmly. "I _tried_ to tell
you about the flak over Romilly."

If only every mission had been so successful, and

if only every flight returned as we returned.  But that
didn't happen.  With my missions, you never knew.  They
could be smooth, or they could be bloody.  Missions number
two and three were quite different, not so much in their
ultimate success against the enemy as in the bloody action
they provoked inside our own B-17.  Many B-17 crews faced
situations outside the official briefing and assurances of
commanders that everything had been taken into
consideration from the moment the crews boarded their
airplanes until the time they landed.  Nothing will go
wrong, they were assured, but things often did.

          I'm a Catholic, so I remember one St. Martin's
day mission very clearly.  The Chaplain, a Catholic priest,
said, "St. Martin always takes care of you flyers."  We
certainly felt much better about the mission because we
were flying into the territory of the "Abbyville Kids," ace
German pilots with many kills to their credit.  The "Kids"
would line up in a long row then streak toward our flight
of B-17's.  At the last minute they would roll over upside
down and go right through us, shooting at the plane in
front of them.  They rolled over because the Focke Wulf was
armored on the bottom.  We could sometimes see our bullets
bouncing off the armor plating.  At the briefing, the
Chaplain then smiled and added, "Besides, the P-47's are

going all the way to the target with you." As much as we appreciated St. Martin and his protection, we felt even better about the Thunderbolts.

On that St. Martin's day, though, all of the P-47's were lost. <u>All</u> of them.

How do you figure it?

An incident on my second raid over Germany, on October 4, 1943, so captivated movie makers that it was another one of those they credited, with mild changes, to the crew of the Memphis Belle. The targets were scattered about in Frankfurt, targets we had been briefed on before and understood very well. Anxious to get on with the war didn't really describe me well enough. My first mission was safely under my belt and I wanted to get the second going.

Several factors combined to bring about the "movie" incident. One, three of our nose guns were malfunctioning when we took off. I managed to repair two of them as we flew over western Germany toward the target, but the third one was out.

Two, it was the first time we encountered fighters firing rockets at us. Since our escort fighters had already turned for home due to low fuel, and new ones hadn't arrived, we were on our own against this frightening

new threat.  Perhaps our gunners, who knew we had one gun
down, were over-anxious.

There was a third factor on this raid, a
situation that burned into my brain until I can still
visualize it very plainly today.  It was the first time
violent death occurred before my own eyes. The man who died
was a German pilot, the enemy.

The one who killed him was me.

Fires were evident in Frankfurt as we approached
the target. Wings ahead of us had done their job, and the
city below was in flames, burning from our bombs and from
the night raids of the Royal Air Force as well.  Frankfurt
war industry and shipping was being blasted day and night.
Along with the other gunners, I was waiting to fight off
the Luftwaffe and their new rockets when the fighters
streaked in.  I could feel the airplane taking hits, but we
were apparently in reasonable condition as we approached
our IP. Then the screaming began.

"Somebody get back here right _now_!  Get _back_
here!  They're _dying_!  Somebody get _back_ here!"

It was, on the intercom, the voice of our radio
operator.  There was still time and the navigator could
handle the guns up front, so quickly I unhooked my oxygen
tube, grabbed up a walkaround bottle, and crawled to the

radio compartment.  Although I couldn't leave my own
station for long, it was obvious something terrible had
happened in the waist of the airplane.  I could see from
the radio compartment that the two waist gunners were
crumpled on the floor, out cold and turning blue.  We were
over 20,000 feet high, the temperature was far below zero,
and their side windows were wide open to repel the German
fighter rockets. They may have been hit, but I could see no
blood.  I got to them and saw that their common supply of
oxygen had been hit and damaged.  They had passed out from
lack of oxygen.  Their ice-caked, blue faces had by then
frozen almost solid. Dragging them to the comparatively
warm radio compartment, I hooked them up to oxygen then
started rubbing them and pounding on them to get their
circulation started.  Once they were breathing, I hurried
as quickly as I could back to the guns at my station in the
nose.

        Talk about things happening quickly, less than
one hundred yards below and slightly in front of our plane
was an ME 110 German fighter firing at a B-17.  The damned
nose guns wouldn't turn down quite low enough, but I waited
and as the German pilot slowly moved forward with a speed
slightly higher than ours, his cockpit came into my gun
sights.  I squeezed the trigger and held it, seeing very

clearly my bullets tearing into his canopy. He must have
been distracted, flying so close below us, and he certainly
must have been surprised, if he lived that long. Parts of
the canopy flew off, and parts of the airplane began to
scatter. Soon he was burning from nose to tail. The ME
110 turned slowly on one wing and began the long fall to
the ground. I saw no parachute, but I'm sure the pilot was
dead.

Hurrying back to my "patients," I continued to
rub them, trying to force blood through their bodies. They
did look a little better, with color other than ice blue
coming back into their faces. Rechecking their oxygen
supply, assuring myself that they were breathing, I
returned to my guns. The sky seemed filled with
parachutes, but our own losses, we learned later, weren't
that bad. Out front, floating downward slowly under a
parachute, was a crewman from one of the high B-17's. He
was close enough to identify the bulky brown, fleece-lined
leather flight suit waist gunners wore. I watched as
another ME 110 circled him slowly, pulled out, then whipped
around and came at him head on at high speed. No, I didn't
actually see the twinkle of light from his wings indicating
machine gun fire, but I will always be convinced that the
German pilot was strafing the helpless man. At that moment

I decided never to bail out.          In another minute I
dropped my bombs directly on the already smoking targets
far below.

          Considering the helpless gunner in the parachute,
what goes around always seems to come around.  Below I saw
a group of four ME's with their wheels down to cut their
speed.  In formation, they were lurking along behind a
lower flight of B-17's, casually firing rockets at the
American planes and doing heavy damage.

          Oh, those Nazis were having a _fine_ time!  They
seemed to be paying no attention to the battles all around
them, intent on their relatively helpless prey.

          Just then, from high up out of the sun, I watched
from my fifty yard line seat as a newly arriving flight of
American P-47 fighter escorts arrived.  The American pilots
quickly surveyed the scene, and took action.  They nosed
over and screamed down on the four ME's.  Within a few
seconds, one of the German fighters exploded, scattering
airplane parts all over the sky.  Before the remaining
three Luftwaffe pilots had time to break away, another
German plane seemed to grow slightly as though it were
being inflated.  Then it merely fell into pieces.  Almost
as quickly the remaining two German planes, with pilots who
had only moments before been thoroughly enjoying

themselves, burst into flames and headed to the ground.
One brown parachute floated behind the four.

No American planes that I could see strafed that
very lucky German pilot, not that they wouldn't have tried.
We were taught that any pilot who was allowed to parachute
alive to the ground could get another airplane, come back
on the next mission, and maybe shoot us down. I remember
one mission where a German fighter pilot was floating down
through one of our formations under a parachute. That is,
I think he was there. The steady flow of tracer bullets,
all converging on one spot beneath the brown parachute,
were so solid that we couldn't even see the pilot. I don't
know if I ever hit one of them, but I took shots at several
Germans under parachutes. Hell, war is war, and the idea
is to kill the enemy.

When we landed on three engines at Bassingbourn,
the two waist gunners I had attempted to help were
evaluated. They would both survive, with frostbite
injuries. I was very happy about that as I handed in my
safety rings from the bombs of mission number two.

Mission number three took off on October 8, 1943,
and the unbelievable action continued.

Speaking of action, we were being <u>bombed</u> from
<u>above</u> on some missions, especially if we were heading for a

target in the German homeland.  German fighter-bombers
would station themselves over our formations before we
reached our target city, then drop bombs in a random and
desperate attempt to hit us before we could hit them on the
ground.  Apparently the German farmers and villagers on the
ground were on their own.

   This was not, of course, an accurate way to bomb,
but occasionally such a bomb would hit an American B-17 or
B-24 in a tightly packed formation, with devastating
results.  Eventually General Curt LeMay spread out our
formations widely. This nearly ruined the German bomber's
chances of hitting one of our planes, but of greater
importance, it made us much more difficult to hit with
anti-aircraft weapons on the ground. Of course it did cut
down on our ability to protect each other, but by then we
had longer-range fighters to help us do that job.

   We were dropping bombs with time-delayed fuses on
certain missions, bombs that would go off well after we
left the target.  Not only did such bombs damage the morale
of the enemy, since he never knew when they were going off,
but it also gave us a feeling that we were helping innocent
factory workers in occupied territories.

   Sometimes such tactics didn't work out so well.
Since the bombs were time-delayed, the enemy could order

innocent local citizens, men, women and children, to remove
them from the target area.  Nobody knew when the bombs
might explode, so only people under the threat of death
would tackle the task of removing them, or allowing their
children to remove them.  We might drop a load of bombs on
a factory in some occupied territory, knowing the factory
workers were really innocents in the big game and thus
giving them time to evacuate the facility before the bombs
exploded.  But then the enemy might simply order the
workers to carry the bombs outside.

We did see strike photos where time delay bombs
seemed to explode in one area some distance from a target,
when we knew we had hit the occupied territory target
directly.  Obviously the enemy had found most of the bombs
and moved them away, or at least ordered the children of
civilian workers to move them away while he watched with
helpless parent workers from a safe distance.

Time delay fuses on bombs served another purpose.
We who dropped them would by then be far from the target,
but the bombs could be timed to explode as a second wave of
bombers was coming in.  Many bombardiers were happy to see
the explosions on the ground as they began to line up their
own bombsights.

Another tactic to try in some way to protect

innocent people on the ground was to precisely time our
strikes on factories to when the worker's shifts were
changing.  In this way we hoped to level the factory just
when one shift had left and another was arriving, possibly
saving a few lives on the ground.  But the enemy,
recognizing what we were trying to do, began to overlap
shifts, offering us no apparent window in which to bomb.

　　　　　Who knows what was most benevolent, and what
wasn't?  We just did our best, but always with the idea of
destroying the target on the ground regardless of cost to
our flights, and to the possibly innocent people down
there.  Certainly many civilian casualties resulted from
bombs that exploded upon contact, and from bombs that were
timed to explode later, or from bombs that missed their
precision target and landed on a school or hospital or old
folk's home nearby.

　　　　　That was war.  We didn't ask for it.

　　　　　I knew what had to be done on Mission Number
Three, and so, once again, did the makers of the exciting
B-17 movie "Memphis Belle."  They liked the action enough
to use it in their film, but they did soften it a bit
because it was truly gory in real life.  Sometimes it got
that way on combat missions.  Our belly gunner was Sergeant
Kerr.  Remember him?  He's the one who challenged the

Memphis Bell crewman lecturing to a group of people on a
bond selling tour.  Here's the real story.

Our target was Bremen, a city we'd studied many
times in ground school, a city our group had visited
several times before.  Never having been there myself, I
was looking forward to the trip.

Flak was scattered as we went in and the few
German fighters who met us were handled very quickly by our
own fighter escort.  Things couldn't have been going better
when suddenly a voice from another airplane began to shout
at us over the radio.

"Your ball turret man is hanging out in the
airstream!" the voice screamed.

Quickly I unhooked my intercom and oxygen, and
worked my way back through the bomb bay to the radio room.
From there I could see that Kerr, who fortunately was
strapped in, had managed to get back in his turret and
right it.  But in so doing, while the turret was
freewheeling, he caught his head in the mechanism.  His
forehead had a terrible, scalpel-like cut all the way
across from ear to ear, and his entire scalp had peeled off
and was hanging down the back of his neck.  He was a
gruesome sight, alright, sitting there unconscious from
shock and cold and lack of oxygen, his turret, still

freewheeling slowly, was spattered with frozen blood.  He
was struggling to breathe, sucking blood into his mouth and
throat, where it then froze into red chunks, further
choking him. The situation was desperate for Kerr.

Outside, a new flight of German fighters had
arrived and were cutting us up, so pilot Bud Evers, who had
joined me in the waist, had to return to the flight deck.
We were also getting hit with flak from the ground, since
this did occur from time to time.  The radio man offered to
help, but I ordered him to stay at his gun while I locked
the ball turret in position so it wouldn't swing down
again. Then began a mighty struggle to pull Kerr up and
back into the airplane.  This would have been tough enough
on the ground, but at high altitude, with flak and fighters
all around, and breathing oxygen from a bulky walkaround
bottle while the airplane bounced around, it was a real
battle.  Quickly becoming exhausted, I could feel my heart
pounding like a trip hammer when finally I gave a mighty
heave and Kerr and I both tumbled onto the floor of the
airplane.

One thing we didn't need was a direct hit, so I
could only hope that the navigator was keeping German
fighters away from our nose.  I jammed my fingers into
Kerr's mouth and throat and began pulling out chunks of

half-frozen blood.  Then I whipped off my mask and jammed
it on his face.  He took a breath of pure oxygen, then
another. I clamped the mask to my face and breathed while I
peeled frozen clumps of blood off his face, then I put the
mask back on him again.  Passing the bloody mask back and
forth between us, I managed to unhook him and drag him into
the radio room and plug in his electric suit.  Then I
skidded his scalp back into position, tied it there with a
strap from a May West life jacket, and injected a shot of
morphine into his arm.  I did check to see that the scalp
aligned correctly, not wanting Kerr to end up with his part
on the wrong side, or with hair all bunched up in one place
on his head.  In fact, I took a few precious seconds to
smooth out the scalp.

Color began to come back into his face. He also
looked a hell of a lot better with his hair where it
belonged across the top of his head.  Finally, I covered
him with a couple of blankets and a flak jacket.

Just as we were turning on the IP to make our
bomb run, I crawled back into the nose and bent over my
bombsight.  It seemed like the longest run in the world as
flak pounded us and enemy fighters continued to attack. I
was also fighting off our navigator, Bruce Moore, who kept
coming at me with a knife to cut my sleeve and a syringe to

give me a shot of morphine.  My face was a bloody mess, and Moore was certain I was badly wounded and bleeding to death right there in front of him.  The blood was from sharing the oxygen mask with Lee Kerr, and I finally convinced Moore of this.

An instant after bombs-away, a Focke-Wulf streaked in and began a roll out to turn toward us. Although he was still some distance out and not expecting firing quite yet, I gave it a try and he burst into flames almost instantly.  It must have been a lucky hit in a fuel line, for he rolled and started down.  Then we passed over and I lost sight of him behind us.

In fact, that cost me a "kill" confirmation and this still irritates me.  From that point on I simply didn't report any planes shot down. To hell with the interrogators. Even Bruce Moore substantiated my claim, but if you didn't see the enemy plane either explode or hit the ground, and you didn't see a parachute, they weren't confirmed, and that was that.

So to hell with all of them back on the ground, asking their questions later.  That German pilot never made it home.  I _know_ that, and that's enough for me.  I finished him myself, personally.  Hurrying back to the radio room, I checked Kerr.  He was still bleeding, but not nearly as bad as before. His breathing and color were good. I stayed with him until we landed, actually sitting astride him during touch down so he wouldn't bounce around. We'd sent up a flare on approach, so an ambulance was waiting for us and he was rushed to the hospital.

Maybe I was a little unhappy about the fighter I didn't get credit for, but I was a hell of lot happier about our belly gunner. He survived to make it home for a long furlough, and with a full head of hair.

Then he returned to fly combat again. He volunteered to fill in as belly gunner on a crew that was one man short. The B-17 took a direct hit, but the crew managed to bail out, and spent the rest of the war in a Stalag Luft. Except for Lee Kerr. He was the only one who didn't make it. He went down with the Fortress, and is now buried in Epinol, France.

I don't know how to figure it.

## Chapter Six   Manny Klette and Other Heroes

There were more heroes in the air war over Europe than you can count.  There were many, many medals awarded to many deserving men and women, some alive and some dead, and this in a war where medals were a little more difficult to earn.  Most ranking officers who served on Awards and Decorations committees, men now retired but who went through the last three wars, admit that with each new war, decorations became somewhat easier to earn.  One retired General in a position to know insists that a Distinguished Flying Cross in the Second World War became a Distinguished Service Cross in Korea, and a Congressional Medal of Honor in Viet Nam.  This is not meant to take anything away from any man or woman who received a decoration, nor is it meant to be controversial.  It is simply the truth.

I received a number of decorations, and I suppose it could be true that my Distinguished Service Cross might have been a somewhat lower ranking Air Medal in the First World War.  But I'm proud of the medals I earned.  On my fourth mission, I was originally put in for the highest award of all, the Congressional Medal of Honor, but I didn't know it.  During interrogation, I was absolutely honest with my answers, admitting to a haziness under morphine, for example. Had I known, I might have been tempted to say I was perfectly sharp and knew exactly what I was doing. Others have done so, understanding the great honor and respect that always follows, with very good reason, the recipient of the Congressional Medal, and why not? That medal is the top, the best, the most prestigious of all. It rates a salute from every other serviceperson, enlisted or commissioned, even Generals. It offers the one who receives it the chance to select anybody, usually a son or daughter, to attend West Point or Annapolis or the Air Force Academy. I'm not necessarily saying I deserved a CMH, but I might have slightly adjusted my answers had I known what they were hoping to hear.

Finally they "reduced" me to the nearly equal Distinguished Service Cross, but they also made the point that I still would have the rare opportunity of nominating someone of my choice to one of the Academies. I haven't done that yet since my sons didn't really want to make a career of the service. In any case, almost every crewmen who flew was a hero, with some of the very few exceptions I'll mention in the next chapter of this book.

Yes, there were plenty of heroes.

Consider, for example, Lt. Addison Baker of

Akron, Ohio, and Major John Jerstad of Racine, Wisconsin.
On the way to the target their B-17 was hit, and soon
flames enveloped the airplane.  Battling the controls, they
continued to the target, dropped their load of bombs, then
died with their crew moments later when their bomber
crashed.

Baker and Jerstad became two of five airmen to
win the Medal of Honor for heroism over Ploesti.

I can think of the young sergeant who was a
gunner on a B-17 during the time I was flying, and who kept
a short diary.  Gunners were special people, highly skilled
and generally enthusiastic about their position.  They took
their job of defending their Fortress very personally, and
enjoyed nothing more than killing an enemy pilot.  They
were all volunteers who would sometimes sleep with their
weapons to keep them clean and dry in the wet English
weather.  This so the guns wouldn't freeze and malfunction
at a critical time in the sub zero temperatures of high
altitude.

This young gunner's diary seemed to capture some
of the heroism, and also some of the resignation, boredom,
and death we came to accept without real acceptance.  In
his diary, the young sergeant seemed to be shrugging his
shoulders and awaiting his own fate.

Parts of this gunner's diary were printed in a rousing book on the air war over Europe called Target: Germany, published by Simon and Schuster in cooperation with Life Magazine in 1943.  Here are some excerpts, exactly as he wrote them.


*June 22 - This was the date of our first engagement. Antwerp, where the Germans were building trucks and tanks, was our target. Our part was a minor one, more or less intended to keep their attention divided, while the main force went to Huls.  It was considered successful.  We were hit hard by FW 190's and had our share of flak.  The two other ships in my flight never returned, taking three of the men in my barracks down with them.  Our tail gunner was killed by the only shot to enter our ship.  He was a fine fellow.*

*June 25 - Today, Hamburg!  Rather a wasted trip. A large formation dropping bombs through a thick layer of clouds which obscured the target.  The flak and the 190's were with us.  One B-17 went down, taking more of my friends and our Operations Officer.*

*June 26 - Target, an airport in Paris, France. No. 1 engine went out over Channel, so we turned back. Others went on in, but weather bad and only a few bombed* target.

      June 28 - Big game, big formation this time. We
made the Germans very well aware of our presence in Saint-
Nazaire. Our bombs raised the submarine docks to heaven.
We encountered clouds of flak and fighters. We left the
fighter opposition shortly after bombing. Some time out
from the target we picked up two German fighters that made
repeated attacks on the tail of our ship. Had the rather
unpleasant experience of seeing 20mm cannon shells
exploding close to our tail. No one was killed or badly
injured. We stopped at an RAF base for the night. They
treated us wonderfully.

      June 29 - Flying today with Lt. L. All enlisted
men in his crew are in hospital, with the exception of one
man who is dead. The trip was without event. We go well
into France looking for our target (an airport) which is
hidden by clouds.

      July 4 - Another Independence Day, quite unlike
any other I can remember. A German aircraft factory deep
within France got a look at some American fireworks in the
form of several hundred 500 pound bombs. Our own crew went
today as spares and had to return just short of France.
Today we have been heavyhearted because Lt. B's crew did
not return.

*July 6 - No mission today.  I received the award of the Air Medal for having successfully completed five combat missions.*

The author of this diary, a young hero in every sense of the word, did not return from his next mission.

In the same book, Intelligence Officers pieced together the following story after interrogating the heroic crew of the famous B-17 "Southern Comfort."  I never flew on Southern Comfort, but early in her missions she earned the reputation of being a "lucky" Flying Fortress, a steady ride that would bring the crew home every single time, regardless of damage.

Here's the story Intelligence put together after post-mission interrogation of the crew.

"We had disposed of six of our bombs when the ship shivered and we knew we had been heavily hit.  The bombardier sent away his four remaining bombs on the docks of Wilhelmshaven before turning to see if the navigator had been killed by the explosion of a 20mm shell in the nose.

"The navigator was alive and uninjured, although the shell had exploded only three inches away from his head and dented the steel helmet he was wearing.  The explosion drove his head down on the navigator's table, which broke under the impact of the helmet.  The only ill effect he suffered was that he could not calculate the course of the plane for about twenty minutes.  During this time the bombardier handled the navigator's gun as well as his own.

"A moment later the right waist gunner phoned; 'Sir, number three engine has been hit and is throwing quite a bit of oil.'  The oil had spread over the wing.  A tongue of flame appeared.  The co-pilot closed the cowl flaps and pulled the fire extinguisher.  The fire went out. The propeller of the crippled engine was now wind-milling and chewing away at bits of cowling.  Sparks were bouncing off the oil-covering wing.

"At this point the pilot noticed that the rudder did not respond.  Presently we found that four square feet of it had been shot away.  When the tail gunner reported the condition of the tail, or rather the lack of it, he also reported that still another shell had burst just in back of him inside the fuselage.

"There was no time to appraise the damage. Southern Comfort had lost air speed caused by the drag of the wind-milling propeller, and an attempt to rejoin several of the formations proved futile.

"It was then that the pilot realized that if we were to return to England we were going to have to do it

alone, crippled and out of formation. The loss of the
supporting guns of other aircraft in the formation was
serious, but more serious was the choice of course. We
flew due north, to put as much sea between us and the enemy
fighters as possible. Meanwhile the Number three engine
was vibrating and the wild prop kept taking bites out of
the cowling.

"We were out over the North Sea when the pilot
announced over the intercom, 'Those who want to, please
pray!' Not long after that we sighted land. We weren't
sure, but we thought it was England.

"As we neared our home base an inquisitive
Mosquito spotted us and finally came so close that we could
see the pilot shake his head at our battle-scarred
condition. He waved his hand and left. Shortly afterward,
we picked up our field."

Southern Comfort landed on three engines with
great holes where the rudder was supposed to be, a
shattered nose section, a wing torn with ragged shrapnel
wounds, and fuselage riddled from nose to tail with flak
and cannon-shell holes. One shell had crashed through the
fuselage directly behind the tail gunner's position,
leaving a gaping hole.

One by one, the crew crawled out, every one a

hero who had not cracked under tremendous pressure and fear.  Not a single one was injured.

But other planes on that mission were not so lucky.  Along for the ride in various B-17's on that same mission were a group of men who called themselves "The Writing 69th."  They were war correspondents from various newspapers back in the states.  One of them, Robert B. Post of the New York Times, a civilian hero who was trying to tell the story as it happened, did not return from that mission.

The "Blue Grass Girl" was a B-17 on her twenty-fifth mission.  The hearts and wishes of all of us were always with the crew of a plane on her final mission.  When Blue Grass Girl took off from her base at Sudbury, the entire Eighth Air Force was with her, in spirit and, for the most part, in fact.  We were hoping her flight would be smooth that February 3, 1945, as we prepared to blast Berlin.

Berlin, Adolph Hitler's home city, was always a tough target, with heavy resistance from the air and the ground.  The city was deep in Germany, but it had to be hit again and again.  More than one thousand fortresses and several hundred B-24 Liberators bombed Berlin that day, blasting Tempelhof Airfield and other targets soundly.

Blue Grass Girl, with Lt. Lewis Kloud in command, was among this great group of bombers, and this was to be her last mission.

It was.

Everything went well for Blue Grass Girl, although the Eighth Air Force took other heavy losses that day. Letting down over the North Sea on the way home and finally passing over the English coastline, the gunners and radio operator of the ship came forward to celebrate their final mission with the men on the flight deck. They were all laughing and shaking hands and generally enjoying themselves as the pleasant, friendly English countryside moved below. They could almost see Sudbury ahead.

Then, suddenly, to the horror of other B-17's in the flight, flames began to appear in the waist windows of Blue Grass Girl. Very quickly the flames engulfed the entire rear half of the stricken Flying Fortress and she began to drop away from the others.

Saddened crews from other Fortresses watched as four parachutes appeared behind the falling, burning Blue Grass Girl. A fifth crewman appeared in the air, but too late for his chute to open and he went in with the burning plane. Blue Grass Girl smashed into the ground and exploded in a field at Church Farm, Raydon, near Southwood.

Later it was learned that the gunners who had come forward to celebrate could not get back to their parachutes after the fire started. Lt. Lewis Kloud and his co-pilot gave these crewmen their parachutes, then went in with their plane.

They were both magnificent heroes.

To fly under the pressure of sadness became a mark of American bomber crews. They flew though they left behind in their huts friend's bunks that had not been occupied the night before, knowing that their own bed might be empty that same evening. Very often they flew with heavy hearts.

One of the real problems faced by the Eighth Air Force in England was re-supplying. When a plane went down, a new plane and crew wasn't immediately forthcoming. When an air or ground crewman was lost, a replacement didn't arrive quickly. This meant empty bunks in the quarters and empty places at the table. The Royal Air Force lived on the credo "full breakfast table" to keep morale up. The RAF filled crews very quickly so men didn't have time to dwell on the empty places, and on friends who had died. This was not possible for Americans, with supply sources so far away. In spite of this, air crewmen maintained a high morale, and were heroes.

Promotions, or lack of them, were a problem. The
Tables of Organization were set up in Washington on a
theoretical basis, and they proved to be quite inadequate
in combat. Sometimes a bomber crew was commanded by a mere
Second Lieutenant well into the mission series. Enlisted
promotions were just as slow to come.

With every reason to become depressed, crewmen
continued to joke and laugh and face death.

"Bless 'em all, bless 'em all." they would sing.

"The long and the short and the tall.

"There'll be no promotion this side of the ocean,

"So cheer up my lads, bless 'em all!"

Yes, they were heroes.

Sometimes a B-17 crew faced an extra demand on
their endless supply of raw courage. During the long wait
after briefing and before takeoff, crews tended to get most
impatient and uptight. It turned to horror for the crew of
the B-17 "Budd's Dudds," a humorous use of the name of
their pilot, Lt. Budd. As their Fortress waited in a long
line to take off for a mission to Magdeburg on September
28, 1944, one of the best-liked ground crewmen, men who
were also a part of the team, attempted to dodge around the
row of idling Fortresses. It was dark and he was hurrying
to his job. He walked into the invisible propeller arc of

Budd's B-17.  He was killed instantly, of course, as the
crew watched.  Their friend was almost cut to pieces.
Although Budd called for an ambulance, the order from the
mission commander in the control tower was "Continue on
your mission. Taxi and take off immediately."

They were heroes.

And so was the ground crewman who was killed.

The August, 1943, raid on Schweinfurt had been a
disaster in terms of casualties, with heavier losses than
the Eighth Air Force had ever suffered on any mission.
Dozens of Fortresses had gone down in flames, carrying
their crews with them.  So when, in October, another
Schweinfurt mission was scheduled, top brass attended each
briefing at each base to suppress any opposition and to
calm fears.  At Great Ashfield, Lt. Col Vandevanter
concluded the briefing for air crews by saying, "This is a
tough job and I know you can do it.  Good luck, good
bombing and good hunting!"

From the back of the room came another voice.
"And good-bye!" it said with a chuckle.  The entire group
in the room, somber until then, broke up in loud laughter.
That crewman, whoever he was, was a hero.

There were so many heroes in that campaign.  The
Chaplains were heroes at each base.  Others who observed

these quiet, committed men as crews kneeled before them to
receive a final benediction before entering their planes,
or who watched them selflessly run an errand to bring an
enlisted man his pipe tobacco, or who watched them sit with
a dying airman in a hospital, holding his hand and quietly
talking or praying, never doubted their great value, their
sincere dedication, or their heroism.

      The heroic British people, battered but never
beaten, had an attitude of kindness and hospitality to
American flyers.  They, themselves, were subject to the
strictest food rationing and other hardships.  They lived
in the dark because of blackouts and in the cold because of
lack of fuel.  Many lived in dampness because of the rain
and fog that came in through shattered roofs. They awaited
with stoic calm the bombs and rockets that would certainly
fall, but who knew where?  They would huddle in shelters or
basements and hear the thunder and feel the shaking, then
they would look out at daylight and see that a friendly
neighbor's flat was no longer there.  Nor was the friendly
neighbor ever going to be there again.

      Yet none of this prevented the average friendly
Englishman from taking in and entertaining any American
serviceman who happened to wander past their door,
especially a flying serviceman.  It was always as though

they wanted very much to honor the American before it
became too late, for him or for them.  They would
frequently offer their guest food in spite of their own
very short supply.  That could include a very rare egg, the
kind you break, not the kind that comes in powdered form.

Sergeant Arizona T. Harris, from Tempe, Arizona,
a B-17 top turret gunner who already had two Focke Wulf
190's to his credit, won his Distinguished Service Cross on
a mission to blast the submarine pens at Saint-Nazaire.
The mission destroyed several pens, but the B-17's were hit
very hard by flak and fighters.  They were caught in a "box
barrage," where German gunners on the ground merely filled
a section of the sky with exploding steel, with radar
guiding their guns.  It was the section through which the
bombers had to fly to reach their target.  Many of the
bombers were hit, then fighters streaked in, and some B-
17's fell from the sky.

On the way back to England, Arizona Harris
continued to battle the attacking fighters from inside the
top turret of his crippled Flying Fortress.  Pilot Charlie
Cramner held the ship at 1500 feet, unwilling to go any
lower because he knew with only two engines left he
couldn't regain altitude if he needed it.  The entire
bottom of the airplane had been peeled away.  The

bombardier and navigator were gone, nobody knew where.

Forty miles northwest of Brest, six more FW 190's attacked, hurtling down on the crippled airplane from high in the clouds. One after another they made passes from behind. Sergeant Harris fought back from his top turret. The order to bail out was given, and two parachutes were seen to blossom behind the struggling Fortress. Obviously, the plane was going into the water.

Momentarily the German fighters paused to circle the parachutists. Nobody knows if they strafed them. Cramner skidded the B-17 down on the choppy water just as the German pilots streaked for another attack. The sea around the stricken Fortress boiled under the rain of bullets from the fighters.

Observers in other B-17's saw something else. The guns from the upper turret were still blazing away at the attacking enemy even as the Fortress settled in the water. The airplane lasted about a half a minute, with the tip of the tail and the top turret the last thing to disappear under the cold waves.

As the dark water closed over it, the guns in the top turret were still spitting bullets at the enemy fighters. Sergeant Arizona T. Harris, a true hero who fought to the very last second, died with his pilot and his airplane.

As much as a piece of machinery could be, the great B-17's and B-24's of the Eighth Air Force were heroes. Horribly damaged, they flew on, bringing crews home under impossible conditions.  I remember a flak damaged B-17 returning from a raid on a German airdrome in July, 1943.  Three FW 190's streaked in for a direct frontal attack. The B-17's gunners destroyed two of the German fighters, and killed the pilot of the third.  This last fighter, with a dead pilot aboard, kept coming and crashed head-on into number 3 engine.  The impact tore off the propeller and knocked the bomber out of formation.  The German fighter, meanwhile, cart wheeled over the Fortress, cutting halfway through the wing and nearly halfway through the horizontal stabilizer.

The ball and top turrets were jammed, the radio compartment was smashed, the instruments, according to the pilot, were "going crazy."  Chunks of metal from the FW crashed through the fuselage.  A German gun barrel stuck itself through the wall between the radio compartment and the bomb bay.

According to observers in other planes in the formation, the severely damaged B-17 then went down.

But it didn't.  It managed to fly on alone, shoot

down two more fighters, and finally make a belly landing at an English base.

None of the crew was scratched.

Lt. Colonel Immanuel J. "Manny" Klette, a commanding officer and friend with whom I flew some risky missions, was a hero. Not necessarily because of the medals he was awarded, though he was awarded many, but because of the job he did. On one of those jobs, in fact, he and I made a controversial and certainly risky decision that also caught the attention of Hollywood movie makers, and became the third incident in the "Memphis Belle" film that belonged to another crew, our crew.

Manny Klette was the son of a Lutheran minister who was born in Germany and immigrated to the United States. As he grew into a man, Manny listened carefully when his father taught him about patriotism, and when his father, who had lived under the boot of it, told of the horrors of Nazism.

Many combat flyers felt that the law of averages would eventually catch up with them. Many felt that only one man in three had a chance of coming through a 25-mission tour of duty. Manny Klette arrived in England as a Second Lieutenant co-pilot in February, 1943. Morale was generally low at that time, since no official "tour of duty" had yet been established. Your combat tour was over when you didn't return from a mission, or when you returned so seriously injured that you were unable to fly again. My friend Klette flew ten missions as Lt. Ed Maliszewski's co-pilot, and when Maliszewski became the first combat crewman to reach the newly announced "25-mission limit" and was rotated home, Klette became the co-pilot for Lt. Keith Conley. He flew eleven more missions with Conley, and although the 369th Bomb Squadron's luck held, they were still getting flak and fighter attacks almost every mission. Once, though, the war came home to Klette, a man who truly loved and valued his aircrew.

On a mission over the Bay of Biscay, Klette made the usual co-pilot's check of the crew by calling each crew member over the intercom. Only the tail gunner, Sgt. Daley, failed to respond.

"Daley?" Klette called again. "Daley, are you OK?"

There was no answer.

Klette disengaged himself from his seat belts and worked his way back to the tail. Ahead in the noisy, narrowing fuselage, over the housing holding the retracted tail wheel, Klette could see Daley hunched over his gun sight. He reached out to put his hand on Daley's shoulder,

but before he could say a word, the tail gunner fell back
into Klette's arms.  Daley was dead with a stray bullet
through his heart.

Manny Klette didn't quit flying missions when he
reached the magic number of twenty-five.  By late July he
was given his own bomber and crew.  He named the bomber
"Connecticut Yankee," and it participated in its first
mission with the airplane of Keith Conley and the rest of
Klette's old crew in the same group.  Conley's B-17 was one
of two lost from the 369th Bomb Squadron that day.

Upon completion of his first twenty-five, Klette
applied to his Squadron and Group Commanders for permission
to fly another tour.  They agreed, but on the third mission
of his second tour Manny Klette was forced to crash land
his bomber in a forest in England after it had taken severe
flak damage over Nantes.  He was critically injured with,
among other things, five bone fractures and flak damage to
his left leg.  During his convalescence, he worked at a
desk, but he kept demanding to be returned to flying
status.

Finally, in July, 1944, he was assigned to
command the 324th "Wild Hare" Bomb Squadron at
Bassingbourn, my home base.

By November, Klette and I were leading the group

together to targets such as the heavily defended oil
facilities at Merseburg/Leuna. Klette had long expressed
the opinion that the creation of a good lead crew depended
upon combat experience, that a lead crew should have at
least ten missions under their belt. Many of Klette's
crews did not have ten missions, and when one of them would
bomb the wrong target, or stumble into a fighter ambush
after wandering off course, Klette would suffer personally,
then reinforce his own training of crews.

He would also fly as regularly as possible
considering his command responsibilities, always selecting
the most difficult targets for his flights. When his own
commanding officer ordered him to stand down and conduct
his squadron duties, Klette ignored the orders and
continued to fly.

I was once asked by our boss, Colonel Henry
Terry, to locate Manny Klette for a conference. Terry was
certain Klette was on the base, for he had once again
ordered him to stand down. I grinned to myself, for that
very morning I had seen Klette in the pilot's seat of a
Fortress taxiing out to take off on a combat mission.

Klette felt that he had to be there. He felt he
had developed methods of avoiding flak and of evading
fighters, and his record seemed to prove it. His mission

total continued to climb past forty, then fifty, and he flew on. His plane took hits, sometimes serious ones, sometimes with me aboard as group bombardier, but he brought his crews home.

In February, 1945, 91st Group Operations officer Lt. Col. Marvin Lord, who had never been to Berlin, asked if he could pilot Major Klette's plane on a mission. Klette resisted even though Lord was a higher ranking officer and an excellent pilot himself. Klette's crew was the most experienced in the group, and he was very protective of them. Manny also knew that where the average number of anti-aircraft guns around any given place might be around eighty, Berlin was defended by more than two thousand anti-aircraft guns. However, the combat mission Lord requested was canceled before takeoff due to heavy weather over Berlin. Since Manny Klette had a dinner engagement in London, he told Lord that in the unlikely event the mission should fly after all, Lord could take the lead position as Aircraft Commander and pilot of Klette's B-17.

The weather forecasters were wrong and after Klette left for London, they rescheduled the mission. Early in the morning of February 3, the squadron of B-17's took off with Lord in command, forming up with other bombers and then heading for Germany. Of the eleven man crew in Lord's airplane that early morning, the radio operator was on his seventy-ninth mission, the engineer on his eighty-first and the ball turret gunner on his <u>one hundred eighth</u>. These men and others had flown with Klette far beyond the required twenty-five. They were the most expert crew in the Eighth Air Force, and all were close personal friends of Klette.

Immediately after "bombs away" over Berlin, Lord's lead B-17 took a direct hit in the waist. The plane was blown apart and tumbled in pieces to the city far below. I will never forget this, for I was in a plane above Lord's plane, and I witnessed the whole terrible drama. Our downward-aimed strike camera also caught the sad action. It was all on the film, the direct hit, the Fortress coming apart, and the broken pieces falling. Klette's entire crew was lost along with Col. Lord.

Manny Klette took the loss of his crew to heart. He felt certain that if he had been there, he could have flown them out of danger by making his usual sharp left turn off target. He became more determined than ever to fly on the most difficult missions to the most important targets.

Crews in the hundreds of airplanes following him

were inspired by his leadership.  They knew that if Klette
was in the lead, the right action would be taken.  However,
our immediate Group Commander, Col. Terry, continued to
fret over his Squadron Commander's appetite for combat.

"We had a rotation policy wherein the squadron
commander would fly when that particular squadron was
leading the group as combat wing or division lead," Terry
explained to author Roger A. Freeman in the absorbing book,
"Mighty Eighth War Diary."

"'Manny' would take his prescribed turns at
leading the group but would also go on missions whenever
his squadron flew.  He did this so consistently I felt he
wasn't paying enough attention to the administration of his
squadron or attending enough staff meetings.  I asked him
to stay on the ground more but he still continued to go.  I
got my dander up and <u>ordered</u> him to only go when his turn
to lead came up.  He still went regularly.  What the hell
are you going to do with a man like that?  He'd give me
that ready smile and all I could do was chew him out and
let him go," concluded Terry, who obviously admired this
squadron commander.

When asked when he was going to quit taking
chances, Klette would answer "When the war's over, I
guess." Klette had learned to live with fear.  He felt he

was needed in the pilot's seat to help win the war.
Klette, who did not quit flying missions until the war
ended, and with an extraordinary mission total of <u>ninety-
one</u>, was a man I admired.  He had no bravado, he wasn't
seeking records, he just wanted to get the job done.

We, he and I, did get it done over Vlotho on
March 14, 1945.  There was a very important eight-lane
railroad bridge over the Weser River deep in the heart of
Germany.  Over this span long train loads of supplies were
rushed to various units of the German Wehrmacht.  The 91st
Bomb Group was flying lead that day, which meant everybody
would drop their bombs when I dropped mine.  It meant that
I would be in command of the aircraft for the bomb run, a
fact that was to become very important as we approached the
target.

Flying co-pilot was Brigadier General William
Gross, the Group Commander.  Flying with the General was a
distinct disadvantage, since Generals usually picked the
tough missions to fly, aware that if they took the easy
ones the press would quickly question their command skills
and even their courage.  So there we were, my friend Manny
Klette in the pilot's seat, the General as co-pilot, Mike
Rheam, from Lewisburg, Pennsylvania, doing the navigating,
and me as the bombardier, heading an entire group of B-17's

to blow up a railroad bridge. Rheam, one of the finest
combat navigators in the war, was responsible for my own
skill at locating and avoiding flak. Mike and I may have
been the worst two spit and polish military men on the
ground in the entire war, but in the air he was a whiz. He
took the time to set up a basic school for navigators, and
I took the course. Mike seemed to appreciate me as a
student since I was the only bombardier who bothered to
enroll. What he taught me saved our ass later, more than
once, so it was really I who appreciated Mike.

In any case, Manny, the General, Mike and I would
have no problem with the bridge, I figured. Of course I
had no idea the mission would result in another cluster for
my Distinguished Flying Cross, and another one for Manny
Klette, as well. If we'd had such an idea, we would also
have known that something was going to happen to bring
these decorations about. Probably something quite drastic.

As we approached the target, everything was
peaceful, at least at first. Our fighter escort was doing
an excellent job of keeping German pilots off our backs.
Then, suddenly, all hell broke loose. From the very moment
the bomb run started, we caught overwhelming flak. Shells
were exploding all around us, and during the sighting
period the black, pulpy smoke was so heavy it was

interfering with my vision. I couldn't see the target
clearly. It was far below, and a relatively small railroad
bridge from that high up. Every time I would sight it,
another group of black flak clouds would obscure it again.
In the movie "Memphis Belle," the director had the plane
flying over a big city rather than a small bridge, and he
had Mother Nature's white clouds blocking the target, but
believe me, it was black and it was flak bursts, although
hazy clouds further down weren't helping the matter.

The closer we came to "bombs away," the worse the
problem became. It was very discouraging to have control
of the airplane, and the entire combat group, and not be
able to make the minute corrections in the bombsight to
center the target. I simply couldn't see it, and I knew
that where I dropped, the others would drop. We could wind
up blowing hell out of the Weser River, or some fisherman's
dock, completely missing the strategically important
railroad bridge and killing nothing but a few schools of
fish. The bridge was down there, but it would be visible
for a second or two, then it would be blocked. There were
also other Fortresses below us, going to and from other
targets in the Vlotho area.

It was mass confusion.

With seconds left to make a decision, with the

airplane bucking about in the sky, I tried one last time to center the target.  Black puffs of flak blocked my view. The navigator urged me to make the drop and get the hell out of there, but instead, certain I was doing the right thing, I made minute adjustments to the bombsight and felt "Klette's Wild Hare" respond by banking slowly to the right.

"What the hell's going on down there?" I heard the General shout over the intercom.  "Why aren't you dropping your bombs?"  Very busy, I didn't take the time to answer.  I knew the mass of airplanes behind were following, and also taking the same punishment we were taking.

"I said, what the hell are you doing down there?" the General demanded.

"Get the hell off the intercom!" I shouted back, continuing the great 360 degree turn over the target.  If Manny Klette, who knew exactly what was happening, had not been with me, he would have taken over the airplane and returned us to a safer course.  He certainly had the authority and the equipment to do it, and both of us knew it. But he was with me, as I knew he would be, and I could almost see him sitting in the pilot's seat, his hands in his lap and a grin on his face, with a very unhappy general to his right.  He agreed with my plan by doing nothing, by allowing control of the plane, and the group, to remain with the bombsight and the bombardier.

During the time of the great circle, I must admit that I was thinking of the previous mission three weeks before, my first after returning from a visit home with Mary.  We had blown the marshaling yard at Stendal to bits. My aiming point had been the engine of a freight train pulling into the yards, and that engine went up in a great cloud of steam and fire.  That and the total destruction of the yard made me so enthusiastic that just for fun, instead of sending the official code words about the strike, I ordered the radio operator to send the expression used by British bombardiers.

After signing a written order for him, he sent the words "WIZARD PRANG" back to base.  Nobody thought it was funny but me, nor did I realize the message would be monitored in London.  They actually fined me $75 and confined me to my quarters for ten days for not following military procedure.  Apparently everybody was on General Gross's case, citing lack of military discipline among his bombardiers. He felt he had to do something.

Oh well, I ducked out of quarters the first night, swiped Henry Terry's car and driver, and took off

for London for the ten days. They didn't think that was
very funny, either, but what could they do, forbid me to
fly any more combat missions? Anyhow, in this case I
didn't announce my ten day vacation over the radio, so they
let me get away with it.

Back over Vlotho we continued our vast circle and
finally turned toward the target once again. This time we
approached from a slightly different direction, and
although the flak was still pounding us, the view of the
bridge far below was much clearer. As the railroad bridge
came into my crosshairs I triggered my load of bombs,
knowing that many planes behind were doing the same. Far
below, I could see some photo P-38's circling to take
pictures.

The photos proved that we completely destroyed
the bridge. In fact, one of the P-38's came up to our wing
and told us that our ship's bombs were the single direct
hits on the bridge itself. The photos even showed a long
and well-loaded German supply train parked on the tracks
just a few yards before the bridge, unable to cross the
great hole we left behind. Apparently that very lucky
engineer had managed to barely stop his train in time.

Back on the ground General Gross called me in to
discuss my military courtesy on the intercom. I told him I

thought it was one of the gunner's who had shouted at him, I didn't know which one. Because the mission had been a rousing success, he chose to believe my story.

Hero Manny Klette, a Lt. Colonel by then with the combat and command experience of a man of fifty seven or sixty seven, was twenty seven years old when the war finally ended and he quit flying B-17 missions.

He recently died of cancer, and we all miss him.

Lt. Charlie Hudson uncovering the top secret Norden Bombsight in his "office" before a bombing mission over Germany. Known then as "Combat" Hudson, Charlie looked forward to the dangerous missions, and eventually became a Lt. Colonel and lead bombardier of the Eighth Air Force in England. When Charlie pressed the button, hundreds of B-17's dropped their bombs.

Once, in command of his B-17 over Germany, he orderd the bomber to "go around" because the target, a railroad bridge of great value to the Nazies, was shrouded in fog and smoke from flak. The entire wing following behind was unhappy, as was a general who was flying as co-pilot. They would all face twice the danger, but Charlie wanted to be sure. This was featured in the exciting motion picture "Memphis Belle."

The crew of "Punchy," Charlie Hudson's first B-17 assignment, was lost on their first mission. Except for the bombardier, Lt. Charlie Hudson (kneeling, second from left), who was left behind that one time. Squadron Commanders assigned a British observer to fill in for Hudson on that photo mission, much to Charlie's chagrin. He felt that no mission should go into enemy territory without a bombardier, a crewman who had several other duties besides aiming the bombsight.

"Punchy" suffered a collision with another B-17 and went down in the English Channel. The entire crew, including the British observer, was lost. Charlie was assigned to another crew, after identifying the bodies found of his friends.

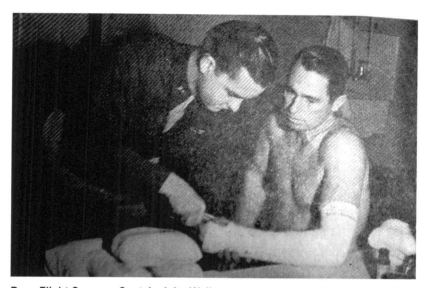

Base Flight Surgeon Captain John Walker removes the cast from the arm of
First Lt. Charlie "Combat" Hudson. Hudson was seriously injured by German
machine gun fire and flak very early in his career as a bombardier. In fact, he
was wounded on each of his first four combat missions, and because of this
was featured in the popular newspaper cartoon column of the day, "Strange As
It Seems." This brought Charlie to national prominence in the United States.
Eventually, two motion pictures were made on the adventures of Charlie
Hudson. These were "Breakout," starring Charles Bronson, and "Memphis
Belle," where several of Charlie's heroic B-17 actions were featured.

General Eisenhower, the Supreme Commander," greets the fake "crew" of the "General Ike."  Some of these men were even under "house arrest."

With Colonel Lord in command as a last minute replacement pilot, the B-17 of Manny Klette suffers a direct hit that blows off one wing. The elite crew was unable to bail out and were lost, along with Colonel Lord. This photo was shot from Charlie Hudson's B-17 "strike camera," and indicates how dangerous, and very sad, bombing missions often were. Thousands of young Americans were killed flying such missions over Germany during World War Two.

Manny Klette, who didn't want to loan out his airplane and who loved his highly trained crew, continued to fly missions and, according to Charlie Hudson, was one of the real heroes of the war. Klette had ninety one combat missions over Germany when the war ended.

Another lonely B-17 with a full crew aboard goes down over Lechfeld, Germany, on July 19, 1944, after suffering a direct hit that severed the entire rear of the fuselage. Other crews watched sadly, knowing there was nothing they could do for their friends, men who would not be laughing and joking with them that night at dinner. Later in his life, Charlie Hudson, who hated the gunners down on the ground trying to kill him, became good friends with one of them after a chance meeting.

Manny Klette, a superb B-17 pilot and one of Charlie Hudson's best friends during the war, flew an astounding ninety one combat missions over Germany. He had the most elite bomber crew in the Eighth Air Force, but the entire crew was lost when Manny allowed another very skilled pilot to fly his plane, with his crew, on a mission. Sometimes it is just bad luck, as Charlie soon realized.

The Klette bomber took a direct hit, the wing was blown off, and the plane went down with all aboard. Charlie Hudson was in the same formation bombing the same target, and sadly watched from above as the Klette B-17 went down.

Author Ross R. Olney (left) and war hero Charlie Hudson. Known during World War Two as "Combat" Hudson, Charlie was the most decorated bombardier in the Eighth Air Force. During his lifetime he was an athlete, pro boxer, oil driller, pro golfer, exotic animal hauler, in a major prison break, defendant in a key drug smuggling trial, and, finally, a lecturer on World War Two and combat flying. For many years he escaped a mob "hit list," though his "grave" is still on the fairway of a popular Southern California golf course (the pro knows where to look for it). The two, as combat vets, became close pals during the writing of this book. Here they look over a model B-17.

Civilian pilot Charlie "Combat" Hudson stands with the beautiful Vultee V1A he
restored in a jungle, then used to haul animals to the United States. The plane
was formerly used by newspaper magnate William Randolph Hearst to fly his
friend, Marian Davies, to her functions.

In "Combat He Wrote," Charlie explains that this airplane was almost junk
when he found it, and how restoration could be done, and how animal hauling
turned into a real profitable business after a hectic beginning

The sleek Vultee V1A Charlie restored to flying condition in the middle of a jungle, then made a wild flight home with a load of exotic animals. There are still airport workers today who will not open the door of a private airplane without positive approval of the pilot, especially airport workers in Southern California. And there may still be descendents of these wild animals in the southern part of California.

Except for the dead monkey that one neighbor threw at another neighbor in a Los Angeles suburb, resulting in a lawsuit that nobody could figure out until this book was published. This was the monkey that a saddened Charlie Hudson tossed out the window of the V1A after being sure that there was nothing that could be done for the poor little animal.

Charlie Hudson, who never stopped seeking adventure in his whole life, and prison escapee Carlos Castro (right), stand by the airplane that Charlie used to fly Castro to Central America after the famous "breakout" of millionaire Joel Kaplan from a Mexican prison. The motion picture "Breakout" starred Charles Bronson playing the role of Charlie, and in the motion picture you can, if you listen carefully, hear Bronson acknowledging "Charmin' Charlie" Hudson.

Bronson did it just to please his friend, Charlie, and it did please him. "Charmin'" was Charlie's civilian nickname, one he used on his restaurants and his golf courses.

## Chapter Seven    Good Guys and Bad Guys and Mistakes

       Combat aircrews in every war dropped things other than bombs.  The crew was taking the same chance, flying over enemy territory exposed to flak and fighters, but they could be on a mission to drop <u>leaflets</u>.  Millions and millions of leaflets have been dropped in recent wars. They might have been official-looking, colorfully printed guarantees to the enemy that they would be well treated if they surrendered, after which they were often shot, anyhow. Or a leaflet could have been a warning to a friend concerning something dangerous about to happen.  Or leaflets may have been mere propaganda, designed to hurt the enemy's morale.

       Here's what one leaflet said, word for word exactly as it was dropped near the end of the Second World War.  This one shows that the Allies tried to be careful in occupied countries.  Tens of thousands of these leaflets were dropped over the affected area.  The leaflet was dated August 26th, 1944. On the front side it said,

**SUPREME HEADQUARTERS ALLIED EXPEDITIONARY FORCE**

**WARNING!**

To the German civilian population in the German
areas West of the Rhine, in the French province
of        Alsace-Lorraine, and in the Grand Duchy of
Luxembourg: The elimination of the German 7th Army
has decided the battle of France.  The survivors
of the Normandy battle and the handful of German
divisions North of the Seine can at best fight a
series of delaying actions on their retreat into
Germany. The German areas West of the Rhine,
Alsace Lorraine, and the Grand Duchy of Luxembourg
     have, therefore, become the rear areas of military
     operations.  Very soon they may become a theatre
of war.

In view of these facts, the Allied High Command
issues the warning appearing on the other side,
to        the civilian population of the regions given
above.

On the <u>reverse</u> side of the leaflet, it said,

1. The rear communications of the remnants of the
German army retreating into Germany will be

*subjected to devastating air attacks. These air attacks will be of the same scope and intensity as the bombings preceding and accompanying the invasions of France. Therefore, whoever lives or works in the vicinity of road, rail or canal communications, or near military depots, camps or war-essential factories, must from now on expect concentrated high-level or low-level air attacks at any hour of the day or night.*

*2. Areas in which there are emergency fortifications (earthworks), strong points and other defensive installations are especially endangered. Civilians working on such military objectives, do so at their peril. In order to avoid needless losses among the civilian population, all civilians are asked to evacuate the above-mentioned DANGER ZONES, and to seek refuge in the country - as far as possible from the Danger Zones.*

*3. Furthermore, the civilian population is informed of the following: all perpetrators of atrocities against non-Germans in these areas,*

*will be brought to trial.  The Allied judicial*
*authorities will accept evidence for such crimes*
*from Germans as well as non-Germans.*

Did people respond to such leaflets?  Yes, to
some extent, and to the extent they were permitted to do so
by the enemy.  Civilians in those days were in a precarious
position.  For the most part, the German military looked
upon civilians in occupied countries as little more than
slaves to do their bidding, whatever that "bidding" might
be.

Of course every army, in every war in history,
had some "good guys" and some "bad guys."  You'll read
about some of our mistakes, and some of our bad guys, in
this chapter.  I'll admit that whereas almost one hundred
percent of all Germans, soldiers and civilians, were
unmitigated shitheels who deserved to die, there did appear
an occasional good German still living.

Consider the story of the German Wehrmacht
Corporal guarding some Luxembourg civilians before their
mass execution, when our bombing was getting more and more
accurate.

"You are in charge of these prisoners, Corporal
Punzel," said a hard-eyed German officer.  "When the firing

squad is ready, bring them out in pairs for their execution." The officer then stalked away.

Punzel, a young German enlisted man, was stunned. The prisoners, he was sure, had done nothing at all. They were a group of civilian firefighters, eighteen men and one woman, who had remained behind to protect their steel factory as the German army approached their hometown, Differdange in Luxembourg. The civilians knew that heavy bombing might burn the factory to the ground. Meanwhile, they were neutral. They were trying to save their jobs, nothing more.

Yet there in the town square German Army Corporal Punzel could see the huge grave that had been dug for the prisoners. They had been accused of sending messages to Allied bombing forces, and it was true that the bombing since the Germans arrived had been very accurate indeed. Very often people on the ground could help those of us in the air to improve our accuracy, especially where our targets were camouflaged. What the Germans were saying could have been true, but Punzel was sure it was not true in the case of these prisoners.

Corporal Johann Punzel listened to the woman crying and the men praying. He thought of his own pretty wife and two young children back in Pressig, Bavaria. He had to <u>do</u> something.

The steelworkers were very lucky that it was
Punzel guarding them.  Johann Punzel was one of those rare
"good" Germans.  First he visited some higher officers and
tried to convince them that the prisoners were innocent.
But it was no use. The front was shifting, and the
Wehrmacht had no time for a matter as unimportant as the
lives of a handful of civilians.  The prisoners were to be
shot for treason.  Punzel was only a corporal, a rather low
rank, and it had been majors and colonels who had ordered
the firing squad.

In an effort to be human, Punzel released the
woman.  He was more frightened than he had ever been in any
battle, but he just took it upon himself to send her away.
After all, the officers had mentioned only "men" prisoners
to be shot.

What about the men?

Risking execution himself, Punzel finally, with
moments to spare, loaded the prisoners in a truck and told
them to leave quickly.  They tried to pay him, they tried
to kiss his hands, but he only said "Hurry!  Please,
<u>hurry</u>!"

It was a small thing in a big war, but Punzel
knew he had to act.  All nineteen were saved and along with

Charlie Hudson and thousands of other veterans, lived to
the peace that followed the war.  To Punzel's great good
fortune, an order to move the entire German regiment came
just as the prisoners were leaving, and his act was lost in
the movement of armies.  The incident was forgotten and he
served with honor, never again disobeying an order.  Punzel
also lived to the end of the war and was mustered out as an
officer, himself.  He had almost forgotten the incident of
the innocent prisoners.

The prisoners didn't forget.  They searched and
searched and many years later found him and invited him to
Differdange, with his family, where he, a former enemy, was
honored.

I won't argue with this.

Did we, the US Army Air Corps, have bad guys,
even deserters?  Yes, I'm afraid we did. It certainly
wasn't common knowledge among the civilian population back
home, and it was embarrassing to those of us who flew
dangerous mission after mission without giving a single
thought to deserting.  Also, it is true that "combat
fatigue" is a real thing.  Sometimes you take so much flak,
see so much blood, watch your buddies being blown to pieces
or burned up, and you snap.  As the young bombardier who
thought he was Jesus Christ in the emotional M*A*S*H

episode turned himself off, so did some of our crews.

At some briefings where the mission was to take us near the Swiss border, we were always warned that there would be extra fighters hovering overhead to shoot down any American bomber heading over the Alps to Switzerland. It was embarrassing, but that is the truth. I've seen entire crews clean their rooms and pack their B-4 bags, each with the full knowledge that one way or the other, the upcoming mission was to be their last.

At the most advantageous time they would veer away from the formation with some words about a flight emergency, then they would head for some airport in neutral Switzerland or some other country. There they would land and be interred for the rest of the war in relative comfort and safety, never to fly another combat mission against the anti-aircraft and fighter planes of Germany. Maybe they even tried to convince themselves that they had a real problem with the plane. Switzerland was certainly better than Germany if you had to land in Europe. For that matter, some crews did have a problem that required them to land as soon as possible, and any neutral country was far better than an enemy country.

In fact, the aforementioned Shoo Shoo Shoo Baby, now perfectly restored and on display in Dayton, Ohio,

finally landed in Sweden after a punishing attack on a
Focke-Wulf assembly plant in Poznan in Poland. "Baby" was
hit so severely that she could fly no more. With only one
engine still functioning, she struggled to Malmo and
landed. After the war, she was sold to the Swedish
government for one dollar. The Swedes converted her into
an airliner and for several years, as "Store Bjorn," she
flew civilian passengers.

Sad to say, by the war's end there were over a
thousand B-17's sitting in Switzerland, alone. They were
all lined up in rows. Many were badly damaged and had been
very lucky, since they were quite unable to fly to safety
in England. Others were in perfect condition, or at least
appeared so from the air.

Only the airplane's crew knew for sure, and they
have to live with that knowledge. Those crewmen who didn't
want to go on that final mission, knowing it was landing in
Switzerland rather than bombing Germany, were told by the
others. They were given the opportunity to go on sick call
that day, or in some other way to miss the mission. No
crewman had to go into exile.

How did massive groups of heavy bombers gather
into tight formations over England without hitting each
other? Sometimes they didn't. Assembly collision was

always a danger in a clouded, crowded morning sky.  I
remember a B-17 from the 398th Bomb Group and a B-24 from
the 392nd Bomb Group assembling for a morning mission on
August 12, 1944.  Altogether there were five hundred
seventy seven heavy bombers collecting together.

The Flying Fortress and the Liberator lightly
touched in the semi-dark morning sky.  Both huge planes
fell to the ground outside Cheshunt in England.  Both crews
were lost, so nobody knows exactly what happened.

Another question was, how did great fleets of B-
17's, all flying as close as possible together and all
firing at enemy fighters zipping about in and out and
through the formations, manage not to hit each other's
airplanes?

The answer?

Sometimes they did hit each other.  In spite of
the training and continual practice of dedicated B-17
gunners, and in spite of mechanisms to prevent a gunner
from shooting off part of his own airplane in the
excitement of an air battle, B-17 gunners did occasionally
machine gun other B-17's.

Consider the amazing story of S/Sgt. Charles
Sibray, a tail gunner on a B-17 flying combat missions over
Europe. The tail gun position was remote from the rest of

Olney 174

the airplane, and the job of tail gunner could be a lonely
one.  One bomber in combat over the target took a direct
hit in an engine and the propeller tore free.  Still
spinning wildly, it ripped and slashed down the fuselage
and finally cut the entire tail compartment off under the
rudder.  The plane flew on, but the unfortunate tail gunner
went down inside the severed tail station.

Once a B-17 tail gunner crawled into his cramped
position under the big vertical stabilizer and rudder, he
was usually there for the duration of the mission.  This
was the case with Charles Sibray in February, 1945, during
a raid on the Ansbach marshalling yard.

"We're shutting down number one," the tail gunner
heard the pilot say over the intercom.  When Sibray turned
to look out through his little side window toward the front
of the airplane, he saw that the number one engine was,
indeed, burning.

"Number one is on fire, sir," he dutifully
reported to the pilot.

"Prepare to bail out," came the order from up
front.  "Stand by for my signal."

According to training, Sibray clipped his chest
parachute onto the harness he'd been wearing, then,
disconnecting his oxygen and other attachments to the

airplane, he crawled from his seat to check his emergency door. From his position behind the tail gunner's seat he saw that he could unlatch and kick out the door, and exit the airplane. With everything in order, he returned to his seat and hooked up to await further instructions. Perhaps the order to jump wouldn't come. They were over enemy territory, and no crewman really wanted to bail out. Maybe the engine fire would diminish, and they could make it home. Sibray looked forward at number one engine. There <u>was</u> less fire than before. He reported this fact to the pilot, but received no answer.

They were very busy up front, he figured, but the fire didn't appear to be immediately dangerous. In fact, it was down to some trailing smoke and little more. Maybe the fire extinguishers had done their job. The Flying Fortress droned on and Sgt. Sibray decided with a sigh of relief that the emergency was over and that they were on their way home. Obeying the strict rule of crew discipline, he remained at his post and refrained from bothering the others with unnecessary chatter over the intercom.

Thirty minutes later Sgt. Sibray observed some flak bursting near the bomber's tail, a fact he immediately reported to the pilot. "We're getting some flak back here, sir," he called over the intercom. "Suggest we begin to evade."

Again, there was no answer. Nor did the Fortress
move one way or the other. It merely droned on, ignoring
the flak, on the course it had been following. Sibray was
becoming apprehensive. He knew the pilot should have tried
to avoid the flak. Maybe the crew had been injured in some
way. The pilot could be alone up front and unable to
respond.

Anything could be happening.

Sibray hooked up to a walkaround bottle of oxygen
and began to crawl forward around the tail wheel housing
toward the waist. When he reached the waist, he was
stunned to see it empty. Both gunners were gone. Sibray
continued forward. There was no radio operator. He
crossed the bomb bay catwalk and opened the door to the
flight deck.

There was nobody there! With a rush of fear,
Sgt. Sibray realized that he was totally alone on the B-17.
Checking the instrument panel, he saw the blinking red
light that indicated the automatic pilot was in control.
He suddenly understood what had happened. During the few
seconds he was unhooked from the intercom, the pilot had
given the order to bail out. The giant airplane had been
flying automatically more than 150 miles over enemy

territory. Looking out the flight deck window, Sibray saw
that the engine was still smoking. He knew that he, too,
should bail out.

Returning to the bomb bay, he dropped out of the
airplane, which droned on overhead. Landing safely in
France, Sgt. Sibray was returned to his base in England by
friendly partisans. Only then did he learn that the rest
of his crew had been taken prisoner in Germany. They were
sure their bomber had long since crashed, a victim of flak,
and that Sibray, the tail gunner, had drifted away from his
friends during their parachute landings.

The fact was, the group had not encountered flak
or fighter resistance that day over Ansbach. After an
investigation, the damage done to the engine of the lost
bomber was determined to have been caused by the accidental
discharge of a .50 caliber machine gun from a Fortress
flying in a wing position.

This was an accident that happened more often
than we wanted to admit, but at least the incidents were
accidents.

Every crewman in the Eighth Air Force wasn't
necessarily a "good" guy, and occasionally one of these
misfits could even pull the wool over the eyes of the
Supreme Commander. Whenever I think of the B-17 they named

"General Ike" it reminds me of a little prick of a
bombardier who for obvious reasons must remain nameless.
He posed with a group of men and General Dwight D.
Eisenhower under the B-17 "General Ike," looking for all
the world like a crewman, which he was <u>not</u> at that time.

Everybody owed this little son of a bitch money.
He came from a very wealthy family who owned a famous chain
of stores. With his money he was able to get higher-ups
under this thumb. Soon most of the others owed him favors,
and he could get advance information on upcoming missions.
Then he would arrange to take the easiest ones for himself,
since the people who scheduled the crews also owed him
money.

I hated his guts because I knew what he was
doing.

On those missions he did agree to attend, he
wouldn't always drop his bombs if he disagreed with the
target. He would merely wait until his plane had passed
well over the target, then drop his bombs on an empty
field. If the flight of airplanes behind him was bombing on
him, they would also miss the target although they might
have had to fly through flak and fighters to get to it,
perhaps even <u>die</u> to get to it. The result would be that
many Allied soldiers might also die because the bomber

hadn't done its job.

Sometimes he would drop, but he would leave the pins in his bombs so they wouldn't explode. That's why, eventually, we all had to turn in the bomb safety-pins on the ground after the mission. This was to prove to the mission commanders that we had dropped "live" bombs.

Strike pictures continued to prove that this bombardier was willfully shirking his duty, disobeying his orders and was, in fact, deserting in the face of the enemy. So as lead bombardier I filed charges against him, including a charge of cowardice in action. Hell, I requested they shoot him with a firing squad. He wasn't too worried about that, feeling sure his family could get him out of the problem, but I managed to get the charges approved by Group and sent to Wing. Wing never forwarded them on to Division, certainly not the part about a firing squad. They did finally discharge the little bastard "without honor."

He probably hated me as much as I hated him, something that happens in wartime, in combat. Your emotions are much sharper, more honed. You love your buddies and you hate your enemies with much more fervor than in civilian life. I thought I had seen the last of him even though I knew he went to work for the Norden bombsight company in civilian life.

Meanwhile, before his discharge and while he was still under house arrest, they brought in the new "General Ike" B-17G for a christening ceremony with her crew. Five star General Dwight D. Eisenhower, the Supreme Allied Commander, the highest brass of all, attended the function, to the great delight of the Army public relations people. But there was a screw-up and the crew who was to take over the airplane was off flying a mission.

In typical Army fashion, the publicity people just scraped up a few guys who were in their quarters, ordered them to put on appropriate clothing, line up in front of the airplane, and to say nothing when the General "inspected" them. Throughout the ceremony and probably until the day he died, General Eisenhower thought these misfits were the crew of his namesake airplane.

When the official picture was taken and sent around the world, Ike was "inspecting" the "crew" which included the errant bombardier.

The war went on. When we landed armed guards always removed the bombsight from the lead plane and the second-in-command and hurried the two top secret instruments to a secure lab where they were serviced and lubricated for the next mission. We always got our "own" bombsight back, and this was important to me because I had built in some modifications on mine. That's how I won my Croix de Guerre from France, in fact.

One day a lab worker came running out. "Major Hudson!" he yelled. "They're taking your bombsight!"

Like hell they were. I rushed to the lab and there he was, the same little deserter, officiously representing Norden and attempting to confiscate my bombsight to take back to the states with him. I argued for a moment, and when I could see I wasn't getting through to him, I simply helped him out of the lab and into his car, all the time with appropriate language to spur him on.

Actually, he was injured enough during the "bum's rush" to have to go to a hospital, but I didn't mind that. I kept my bombsight.

Oh, and I had to write a letter of apology that went into my record. It wasn't to him, but to the WAC driver he was using. Apparently my actions and admittedly strong language had truly offended her. I wrote the letter. So what?

Not that things that happened in the service didn't often help or hurt your life later, in civilian life, like this did him. While I was training in bombardier school, I played golf with many civilians,

especially rich civilians like industrialists and other
millionaires.  It was "in" at that time for them to pay
attention to young servicemen, and I was a hell of a golfer
besides.  One time I enjoyed some games with Billy Pabst,
of the famous Pabst Blue Ribbon brewing family.

These pals from civilian life would often send
gifts to us overseas.  They kept in touch.  So when I came
home as a "hero" to go on a bond-selling tour, I went to
see these same millionaires.  They were very responsive and
I managed to sell them more than eight million dollars
worth of Government savings bonds, actually an excellent
investment for them.

During one of these visits, Billy Pabst said, "If
I can ever do anything for you, Charlie, let me know."

Much later, after the war, I was running a bar in
my home town of Taft.  But there was a serious beer
shortage.  Not a bar in town had any beer to sell.  So I
called Billy Pabst.  I figured, what the hell, it can't
hurt.

"Billy, you said if I ever needed anything, to
call you, right?" I said to the beer baron.

"I did say that, Charlie.  What do you need?"
Pabst responded.

"Beer," I answered.  "Do you suppose you could

get me a few cases of beer for my bar?" I asked.

Pabst considered for just a moment. "Do you have a railroad station in Taft?" he asked.

We did have a station, and I said yes.

"Is there a siding there?" Pabst asked.

"Yes," I answered.

Within a few days a box car arrived and was sent to the siding, where it was parked. It was jammed to the doors with cases of Pabst beer. It was an entire <u>box car load</u> of beer. Every few days I would go to the box car and take cases of beer to my bar. My local Pabst beer distributor was fit to be tied, because he couldn't get any beer at all. I was the only bar in town to have beer, thanks to Billy Pabst. By the time I got through the carload of beer, the beer shortage in Taft was over.

One more thing. I tried several times to get Pabst to bill me for the 75,000 cases of beer.

By orders of Billy Pabst, the Pabst accounting department never would, and never did, send me a bill. All I got was a note from Billy. "You did your part, Charlie," it said. "This is how I want to say thanks."

This section of the book, with misfits, screw-ups, and other random stories seems a good place to talk about missing the target. It happened to me, especially on

Mission Number Seventeen to Metz/Frascaty Airfield at
Avord, France, on April 28, 1944.  This one stands out in
my mind because our pilot, Captain Bob Roberts, and our co-
pilot, Colonel Putnam, were both flying their final
missions.  We were leading the entire Wing on this one, so
many other bombers were going to drop when I dropped.
Fortunately, over one hundred P-47's and over eighty P-51's
were assigned to protect us, and they came in handy.

Assembly was smooth, the trip across the channel
and into France was uneventful, the target was visible from
the I.P. and I had a beautiful bomb run.  My crosshairs
were exactly on the huge headquarters building of the
occupied airfield.  On each side of the building was a row
of hangars being used by the Luftwaffe.

Then things began to go wrong.  I couldn't get a
good connection with the airplane out of my bombsight, so I
had to ask Bob Roberts to fly a manual bomb run.  Finally I
dropped the bombs, but they totally missed the headquarters
building.  They did drop along the row of hangars,
destroying some of them, so it wasn't a total loss.

Accurate flak made it necessary to take evasive
action, but the instant we left the flak field about thirty
fighters jumped us.  They made only one pass, and I got off
a hundred or so rounds at them with the chin turret, then a

flight of our Mustangs streaked in and the Germans went home.

After we landed and according to strict tradition for those finishing their missions, Col. Putnam and Bob Roberts were grabbed by the crew, dunked into a huge tank of water, and then rushed away dripping wet by top brass for a final interrogation. We may have missed the primary target, but the day was a good one for Putnam and Roberts, and our bombs did hit the enemy.

In yet another very tragic screw-up, American Commanding General McNair was killed on the ground on July 25, 1944, by a group of American bombers. It was on my twenty-fifth, but certainly not my last, combat mission in B-17's. We were trying something that needed a high degree of precision, saturation bombing in direct support of the US First Army in the Periers-St.Lo area. We were to bomb only a thousand or so yards ahead of our front line troops on the ground. Despite every precaution to ensure there would be no "short" bombing, one hundred two soldiers on the ground were killed, including Gen. McNair, and three hundred eighty were wounded. We also lost five B-17's on that mission.

I am absolutely certain that my own bombs hit exactly where they were supposed to hit, and so did the bombardiers dropping when I dropped. I saw them blowing the enemy to hell. But as we were approaching the target, a group of B-26 medium bombers pulled into formation ahead of us. Below, the front lines were so close together that it appeared some of our troops were in hand-to-hand combat. The lead B-26, we learned later, had a bomb release malfunction. When the bombardier opened his bomb bay, his entire load of bombs accidentally dropped. His whole group did as they were trained to do, and dropped their bombs. Every bomb fell short of the target, into our own troops.

It's bad enough to be wounded or killed by the enemy, but it's a hell of a thing to be wounded or killed by your own Air Force.

It was over. There was nothing anybody could do. I took a break back home in the States, a reward for flying twenty five missions, and then requested to be sent back to Bassingbourn to fly more missions.

Of course, although Mary strongly objected, the brass granted my request.

## Chapter Eight  The End of the Conflict

It took the Eighth Air Force until the early
Spring of 1943 to introduce the 25-mission limit for bomber
crews.  Before that, crewmen had to either die, be taken
prisoner, or be injured so severely that they could no
longer fly.

Or they flew combat missions.

Crews understood that their chances of flying
combat forever were slim.  It was possible, of course, that
a crewman could fly hundreds of missions, all the way to
the end of the war, and never get hurt.  But it was very
unlikely.  So morale was low until the twenty-five-mission
limit was announced.

Not that in the long run and except for a few
unlucky ones who died on their twenty-<u>sixth</u> mission, it
made all that much difference.  The war in Europe was
grinding down, the war in Africa was going more smoothly,
Italy was in deep trouble, and the war in the Pacific,

though none of us at that time could foresee it, was due to
end in a blinding flash of atomic light.

You could always figure, though, that somebody in
Washington was going to screw things up for somebody on the
front lines, and they did. Within a year, due to better
skills, better technology, better fighter protection and
other things, attrition among air crews - make that killed
or missing in action - had halved. So, according to
Washington, every crewman's chance of surviving was
doubled. Naturally, the Washington desk troops jumped in
with this new knowledge and issued another decision in
April, 1944, to raise the limit to thirty missions.

They did allow, with morale in mind, that men who
had already completed fifteen or more missions would be on
a sliding scale. The nearer a crewman was to the magic
twenty-five, the fewer missions he would have to fly over
twenty-five.

Never a desk-set to leave well enough alone, it
became evident to Washington that aircrews were
comparatively safer on missions after, and in support of,
the June 6, 1944, invasion. So in their great wisdom and
the mighty knowledge of combat conditions they gained while
sitting at a desk in Washington, they decided to extend the
number of required bomber missions to thirty-five before

rotation.  A fighter pilot's tour of duty was raised from
200 to 300 hours of combat flying.

It was difficult for the guys flying the
missions, and getting shot up and shot down, to accept that
they were safer than before.  They figured Washington must
have known something they didn't know and in fact, many of
them fervently wished that the officers in Washington would
leave their desks and come over and fly a few combat
missions.

Washington heard them talking.  In what seemed
almost to be vengeance, and certainly in what was a full
circle, the deskbound officers back home finally determined
that combat crews would fly an _indefinite_ number of
missions or hours, as long as they were "mentally healthy."
Only when it could be determined that a crewman was
suffering from combat fatigue could he be taken off
"operational" flying, which meant combat flying.  The
circle was completed in late June, 1944.

Fortunately, combat officers in combat zones were
more sensitive to combat problems than were their rear
echelon counterparts.  Washington said that only Group
Flight Surgeons could certify when a man was too tired to
fly anymore, so front line combat medical officers
determined that this could be found in most airmen, by a

stroke of coincidence, after the recently-abandoned thirty-
five-mission limit. It just seemed to work out that way,
according to command officers who knew about combat.  Under
no circumstances, in fact, could a man's fitness-to-fly-
combat-physical-exam be put off beyond that limit, unless
he requested it.  In almost every single case, a crewman
with thirty-five missions was found by combat-zone flight
surgeons to be fatigued and no longer able to fly combat.
Sometimes this was even determined without a one-on-one
exam.  Combat medics were so good they could merely look at
a crewman's records and see that he was too tired to fly.
Airmen were encouraged by local flight surgeons to think of
the thirty-five mission physical as a combat mission limit
in fact, and that's how it worked.

        Of course none of this affected me very much,
though I was still flying combat. I had requested my tour
of duty be extended beyond the original twenty-five, and it
wasn't all "blood and guts."  We had fun with each other,
and fun with the civilians back home.  When we visited home
on furlough, people would ask us to write down their names
so our crew chiefs could chalk them on bombs to be dropped.
A picture would be taken before the bomb was dropped to
send home to the people named.

        One oil field guy by the name of Brewster, a guy

we called "Baggy Drawers" although he hated the term,
wanted his name on a bomb.  Back in England, I mentioned
the nickname to my crew chief, and that's what went on the
bomb.  It was a present to old Adolph Hitler from Baggy
Drawers Brewster back in California.  The problem was, the
bomb hung up in the rack, and I nearly fell out of the
airplane working it loose.  The story was picked up by the
media, and finally wound up in the popular newsletter
printed by Standard Oil for their workers in the Taft
fields.  It was all about the hung-up bomb with the name
Baggy Drawers Brewster on it.

      Brewster wasn't all that happy about it, but on
the other hand, he wasn't all that distressed either.  One
thing for sure, he knew "his" bomb made it to Germany.

      My last combat mission, number thirty-seven, was
flown on April 15, 1945, just before the war in Europe
ended.

      Everybody my age, and even a few youngsters,
remembers that at Reims, France, on May 6, 1945, an
important document was signed in a little schoolhouse.
German Grand Admiral Karl Doenitz, speaking for a dead
Adolph Hitler, an evil dictator who had killed himself
rather than face certain execution, signed an unconditional
surrender of all German troops.  The world's bloodiest

′ conflict till then was ended.

Sitting in the nose of the airplane on that day in April three weeks before the momentous surrender, returning to Bassingbourn after a maximum effort mission to help clean out some coastal gun crew pockets of German resistance around Bordeaux, France, I grinned at how Col. Henry Terry, flying as co-pilot, had been "educated" that day. I had developed a technique of avoiding flak, and had been using it for some time. It involved gentle, ten degree turns from the IP all the way in to very near the target. I'd turn the airplane very gently ten degrees to the right, then ten degrees to the left, and the group behind us would obediently follow. Looking back, you could see the flak bursting where we _should_ have been, not where we _were_. I asked Col. Terry how he liked my flak-avoidance system.

"I love it," he said with a grin. "I never saw it done before, but I _love_ it!"

I taught the technique to other bombardiers, and before long the whole Eighth Air Force was using it.

Sitting there in the nose on my final mission, I knew that the great war to end all wars was nearly over. Of course the Japs were still active in the Pacific, but I didn't imagine they would be much of a problem with Hitler

dead, Italy's posturing, egotistical Mussolini strung up by
his own people, and the Axis crumbling.

How would I handle civilian life, if that's where
my destiny took me?

Or would it be the Pacific theater of operations
for me?  Could I live without the action I'd become
accustomed to, even grown to love, and the men with whom
I'd become so close?

Thinking back on some previous missions, I
attempted to capture my feelings as they were then, nearer
the beginning.  Was it possible that in the thick of things
and in spite of the fear, I was enjoying myself?

On May 24, 1944, I had a good look at the very
center of the "Big B," old Adolph's home town of Berlin at
the time though he, of course, was living deep under ground
for safety. Fredrickstrasse Station, in downtown Berlin,
was our aiming point, and we were leading the entire Eighth
Air Force.  Bud Evers was the pilot, John Davis the co-
pilot, Bill Borellis the navigator, and we had an
experienced gun crew.  We were higher than a kite that day
after briefing.  We couldn't <u>wait</u> to go.  What made the
mission sound even better was the intelligence part of the
briefing that insisted Hitler had his crack gunners
defending other, more strategic targets, and that only

women and children were manning the anti-aircraft guns in
and around Berlin.

After bombs away I could see the city exploding
and burning fiercely below, entire buildings crumbling into
littered streets.  Thousands of Berliners died on the
ground that day.  The mission was declared a ninety percent
success, which meant a smashing success.

It had been no milk run.  The gunners on the
ground were far more accurate than we'd been told to
expect, and we lost several Fortresses.  But it was no milk
run for them, either, whoever they were.  That night
hundreds of "unskilled" women and children anti-aircraft
gunners didn't make it home to their beds, nor would they
ever again.

The absolute terror of the mission over
Lutzkendorf, Germany, came to my mind there in the nose of
the B-17 returning from Bordeaux just before the war ended.
Our target that day was an oil refinery.  There were huge
storage tanks strung out in a long row following the gentle
contours of the land for more than five miles.  Movie-maker
Cecil B. DeMille couldn't have produced a more spectacular
effect as one of our lead bombs, perfectly aimed, went
directly into the first fat tank in the long row.  The
massive, loaded-to-the-roof storage tanks exploded one

after another, beginning with the first and going down the
long meandering line in an atomic-like domino effect, each
one shooting a great column of flame thousands of feet into
the air as it ignited the next one. Although we were at
20,000 feet, the airplane shook as though it had been
directly hit with flak as each tank detonated. It was
frightening and exhilarating at the same time, a hypnotic
spectacle of tremendous destruction that held us nearly
spellbound.

Somehow, in spite of all the people who died in
the air and on the ground during all the other missions,
this one impressed upon me the tremendous and terrible
power we had in our Flying Fortress.

The "Wizard Prang" mission always comes to mind,
even today. That was when my Fort led a vast armada of <u>two</u>
<u>thousand airplanes</u> on Stendal, Germany, on March 23, 1945.
The damage done on the ground was greater than any
hurricane, any tornado, any flood, anytime in history, as
thousands upon thousands of heavy bombs and incendiary
bombs and fragmentation bombs destroyed everything and
killed everybody within range.

I was proud to have dropped the first bomb.

In vivid, sad detail I thought of the broken,
burning and somehow very, very lonely B-17 Flying Fortress

far below as it staggered across my bombsight viewfinder on its way to death on the ground.  I was zeroing in on my aiming point in Lechfeld, Germany, on July 19, 1944, when the falling plane drifted slowly across.  The deep sadness we always felt when a plane went down seemed magnified in my heart by the lens of my bombsight.

That B-17 looked so alone down there as she traversed the field of view, falling, burning, her crew, my friends, still aboard.  I so much wanted to help her, and them, but I couldn't.

The unimaginably vast armada of ships in the English Channel and on the coast of France after the D-Day invasion stood out in my mind as I think back. I saw the armada as we flew over on an invasion-support mission to Bordeaux, France, on June 19, 1944.  This was my first mission after the invasion, and it was difficult to believe the astonishing number of ships ferrying troops and supplies back and forth between England and the beaches of France on the continent.

Watching with dread the German V2 rocket screaming up at us on April 24, 1944, over Erding, Germany, was chiseled into my memory and came to my mind that day on my way home from my final combat mission.  The huge rocket I spotted as it left the ground on its way to England

seemed to me to have the name MAJOR CHARLIE "COMBAT" HUDSON
painted on its nose.  It streaked higher and higher,
appearing to alter its course slightly to head directly for
our B-17.  I was fascinated by the huge, deadly machine as
it drew closer and closer.  The Germans would have been
very happy had their rocket hit a B-17 by accident, but at
the last minute the V2 seemed to veer away and head across
the channel. I hope it didn't kill anybody on the ground.
I'm very glad it didn't kill me.

There was something else about that Erding
mission, though I didn't know it at the time.  Many, many
years later, when I was running a successful restaurant in
Oxnard, California, (named "Charmin' Charlie's" by my sweet
wife, Mary), I met a local businessman who was attending a
meeting in our banquet room.  We chatted and gradually some
of our past came out.

"I flew as a bombardier over Germany in World War
Two," I mentioned.

"Oh, really.  I'm of German descent and lived in
Germany during the war. Where did you bomb?"

"Oh, Berlin and Frankfurt and other big cities,
and some small towns I'm sure you never heard of," I
answered.  The V2 mission came to mind again, after all the
years.  "One of them was a little town by the name of

Erding."

He was thunderstruck. "Erding? I was in Erding during the war, during the bombing. I was an anti-aircraft gunner," he exclaimed. "What date?"

I gave him the date of the Erding mission, and after more conversation, we both realized that he was on the ground between two hangars on our target airfield, his gun position easily visible in our strike photos. He was manning one of those very accurate anti-aircraft guns. "You didn't hit the airfield, but some of your bombs destroyed my home," he said.

"Some of the planes may have missed, but my bombs did hit the airfield directly," I argued, "and you managed to hit my plane pretty hard that day."

"Thank you," he responded politely, "that's very nice of you to say," and Karl Eichner, once an enemy who tried to kill me as I was trying to kill him, has been my friend ever since.

On April 18, 1944, we bombed Oranienburg, Germany, a little town on the outskirts of Berlin. It was my thirteenth mission and I thought about it again coming home from that final, thirty-seventh mission. On the way in to Oranienburg the cloud cover forced us to reduce our altitude. This meant that I had to quickly re-figure everything in the bombsight, a task I managed to accomplish just a moment before it was time to open the bomb bay doors. Everybody behind us was waiting to bomb when we bombed, waiting and watching for me to open my doors, so the last minute pressure was intense. It was going to get even more intense.

The bomb bay doors didn't open electrically, and very quickly a tight situation was becoming an emergency. We tried to call the deputy leader on VHF. Since he also had a bomb sight, he could take over, but we couldn't reach him. There was no time left for somebody to go back and crank the doors down. With a sigh and a prayer, I proceeded to do the only thing I could under the circumstances. I reached for the emergency salvo release, a handle on a B-17 that was supposed to unload all the bombs when the job had to be done in a big hurry. The emergency salvo release mechanically dropped open the bomb bay doors and released the bombs all in one motion, by means of a cable and pins connection. If it worked. If it malfunctioned, then nothing at all would happen.

By edging the handle forward very, _very_ slowly and carefully, and with advisories from the radio operator who was watching the bomb doors for any movement, I reached that point at which the pins holding the bomb doors pulled out and they fell open, but not the point where the bombs would salvo.  Those pins were still in place, a bare fraction of an inch from pulling out.  If they had pulled, then all the others behind would have dropped their bombs as mine dropped, and the result would have been useless if not chaotic.  The planes behind us obediently opened their bomb bay doors when they saw mine fall open.  Outside, the temperature was thirty-six degrees below zero, but I was dripping with sweat.

Realigning the bombsight, I brought the ship into position so that the target was in the crosshairs, then I nudged the emergency salvo release lever forward that extra fraction of an inch.  The bombs dropped away, and so did bombs from all the other ships.  We hit the target squarely.

My problems weren't over on that mission.  Our pilot, Bob Roberts, called to say that the open bomb bay doors were holding us back.  Closing them, as I've said before, was my job, and they wouldn't close electrically just as they wouldn't open electrically.  Using two walkaround bottles of oxygen, I crawled back and cranked the doors up by hand.  By then the tips of my fingers were frozen solid. Thanks to Sgt. Neale, the top turret gunner, who allowed me to put my hands under his electrically heated suit, my fingers thawed and were saved.

They were hurting so bad on the way home that I didn't even notice the terrible flak bursting around us. That mission is burned into my memory.

There were others, some more difficult, some easier, but none completely routine. The last B-17 mission of the war was flown by another crew on May 6, 1945. It was a leaflet mission flown by the 306th Bomb Group over targets in Germany. Twelve Fortresses took off on that mission to drop hundreds of thousands of leaflets telling German civilians what to do since Germany had surrendered, and assuring them that their children wouldn't be massacred by American soldiers, as the Nazi Gestapo had promised them would happen.

Twelve B-17's returned from that last mission, and that is as it should be. It was, after all, a mission of mercy, not of death.

By then it was nearly over for me, and with some misgivings about returning to civilian life but anxious to see Mary and my friends back home, I waited only three more days for my orders to be cut. I planned to return to the oil fields, a job I really loved, and I hoped to open a little bar somewhere on a part-time basis. I also wanted to sharpen my golf game again, maybe even tour. My war

injuries had healed, and I was scarred but really no worse
for the wear.  I should have stuck to these plans rather
than to reach for more adventure.

That period of time did give me a chance to talk
with the First Sergeant about a fund of money we kept in
the Group.  Officers had been donating twenty shillings
every pay period, enlisted men ten. Nobody ever refused to
kick in their share and by near the war's end there were
many thousands of dollars in the kitty.  What was it for?
It was used to pay eight hundred dollars to each woman who
was found to be pregnant by one of our men who had since
been shot down.  Eight hundred American dollars in those
days would pay for the birth, and most expenses to get the
child off to a good start in life.  Eventually, what was
left in the fund was donated to Army Relief but that wasn't
what the sergeant and I discussed.

To be sure no mistakes were made, the pregnant
woman had to bring in her church Vicar and other witnesses
and meet with a board of our people.  English people
weren't uptight about sex, and the discussion was always
very frank and quite sexually explicit, even with the Vicar
present.  English women seemed to have little problem with
discussing various body parts, and how they functioned
together on that special and very fruitful occasion.  The

lost guy's buddies were brought in as witnesses, figuring
that most men tended to brag about their conquests. A
decision was made and the money more often than not
awarded.

There was this one sergeant who had been seeing
an English girl regularly. He stayed over with her one
night and the two slept together and enjoyed each other
sexually. Then, when his girl friend went to work in a
parachute factory the next morning, he nailed her younger
sister who had joined him in bed. This may not have been
exactly moral, but it happened, and the sister went happily
off to school. In a physical feat of strength and sexual
endurance we still talk about, the young sergeant then
serviced the <u>mother</u> of the two girls.

A few days later, he was shot down.

Before long the three women came in and reported
themselves pregnant, all by the very same sergeant. They
asked to pick up their money, and that is what the fund was
for. There seemed little doubt that the healthy and lusty
sergeant had accomplished the miracle, so they were paid
off.

That could have ended the story.

But it didn't.

Three months later, after having hiked all the

way through the Pyrenees Mountains, the sergeant showed up at Bassingbourn. He was flabbergasted, but agreed that he probably was the father of all three. Eventually, he married the original girlfriend, and stayed in England to live. I don't know what English law is, but I suppose he adopted the other two children.

In any case, he must have had a fascinating family life for years to come.

My orders arrived, and I headed for home. Not that it was all that simple, and not that I had the slightest idea what escapades awaited me, exploits on <u>both</u> sides of the law. I knew, of course, that I would be welcomed home as a conquering hero, and that was fine with me. My decorations had been earned the hard way, in fear and pain and sometimes desperation, especially my Purple Hearts. I had been in the right place at the right time to help others survive, and had possessed the presence of mind to <u>do</u> something. I looked forward to what I knew was coming, and hoped it would last for awhile, and that Mary would enjoy it, and that my old pal and second father, Orville Hall, and his grown son and my friend, Donald, would be a part of it and enjoy it as well. I had no idea what Orville had been doing in the meantime, on my behalf and with regard to my future.

Bassingbourn was chaotic those last few days.
Whole Wings were there one day and gone the next. We flew
our B-17's to Boston and handed them over to the Army, then
I climbed aboard a troop train headed for Beal Army base in
Northern California. The train plodded along a hitch or
two above a cattle train, and our car was as hot and packed
as a horse car. It was a miserable trip when you consider
the train was packed with men anxious only to get home. I
had almost decided to head back for more combat when we
finally arrived at Beal. Absolutely typical of the Army,
when I stepped off the train in California they handed me
orders for Sioux Falls, North Dakota.

Fortunately, there was a thirty-day furlough
thrown in, so I crawled on another train and headed for
home. Mary and Orville picked me up in Bakersfield, drove
me to Taft, and we began a round of parties with the old
gang. It was great for thirty days, but I was ready for
Sioux Falls. When I arrived there, I learned that the Army
had decided to send all officers above the rank of Major to
a Japanese training school in North Carolina. With the war
in Europe over and men returning to the states in droves,
there was a lot of confusion. I was a ranking flight
officer and was given command of our group which wound up,
again in Army fashion, at McDill Air Force Base in Tampa,

Florida.

        Tampa, infamous as "one a day in Tampa Bay," had changed.  The base was a relatively tight military installation although everything was in a state of flux.  I was commanding over four thousand soldiers who, as the war neared an end, were a troublesome mob anxious to go home.  After V-J Day, after our ignored warnings to Jap civilians, after the atomic bomb that flattened Hiroshima was finally dropped by the B-29 "Enola Gay" on August 6, 1945, military discipline deteriorated even more.  I was at loose ends myself, and tried to think up ways to ease the boredom.  My old buddy and long time friend, navigator John Wallace, had simply walked away and headed for Indianapolis, his home town, to wait out his discharge.  He knew that discipline was lax, and that he was probably on solid ground, and he had certainly done his part over Germany during the fighting. Technically, John was AWOL, Absent Without Official Leave, but he wasn't worried. I tried and tried to get him to come back to Tampa, for an "official" discharge, but he ignored me.  So I sent him a formal and very ominous-looking telegram signed with the name of the officer in charge of courts martials.

        REPORT TO TAMPA AIR BASE TOMORROW, OR FACE IMMEDIATE COURT-MARTIAL

John reported the next day, and we had a <u>great</u> party before I handed him his discharge papers.

The thousands of men awaiting discharge regularly tore up Tampa. I was spending most of my days sitting on court martial boards, an unhappy duty. Nor could I find it within myself to hand down Dishonorable Discharges, Bad Conduct Discharges or other major punishments to men who had served honorably, then committed a "crime" because they were bored. These men with whom I had flown, men who lived through hell and who were at that time only awaiting discharge, were no longer real soldiers. They were civilians still in uniform. In fact, I admit that I regularly sent my own best buddies to the discharge section first, a department that said it could only handle about twenty-five a day. We changed that pretty quickly.

Meanwhile, the men still waiting raised some hell in Florida in their anxiety to get home. The trouble was, I'd handle each situation by sending them to the discharge line rather than handing them any punishment. By the time somebody in the military police realized a soldier should be going to jail, that soldier would be a civilian. Before long the word was out. "If you want Colonel Hudson to send you home honorably, go steal a car or break in to a liquor store and throw a wild party. Get into some <u>trouble</u>!"

The honorable discharge rate kept climbing,
though things were getting out of hand. Hell, I never
claimed to be a really serious soldier myself. From a
couple of dozen a day, the number rocketed to nearly three
hundred fifty every day, and to my knowledge none of these
guys ever caused trouble back in civilian life, back with
their friends and family and back on their old jobs.

That was another thing about WW II that might be
difficult to believe today. Your pre-war job waited for
you. No employer would have had the guts or the total lack
of common sense to turn you away when you finally came
home, even if it had been years. He would have been strung
up. He would have been ostracized for being a goddamn spy
or Nazi-lover or something. I never doubted for an instant
that my old job in the oil fields wouldn't be there when I
got home, though I never really discussed it with my old
boss.

Those who were not discharged in Tampa, or who
happened to be AWOL when their name came up, or who had
various combat related problems, were ordered to hospitals.
The streets of the base were becoming deserted, the mess
halls empty. I was getting anxious to get going myself, to
stop in New York to visit my pal and former commanding
officer, Henry Terry, and then to head for home to Mary.

Finally the last man was discharged from the Tampa group.  I cut my own discharge orders, handed over command of the base to a skeleton crew of men, put out the cat, turned off the lights, locked the doors, and headed for New York.

I was <u>Mr.</u> Charles S. Hudson again.  <u>Lt. Col.</u> Hudson was in the history books, for whatever he and they may be worth.  All I wanted was to go home.

I didn't know what was ahead for me, but none of us can ever really know that. But if I had known the amazing twists my life would take, would I have changed anything?

Hell no!

## Chapter Nine   Charlie Hudson Day

Taft, California, a great place to live, will never be compared to New York City.  Taft is not a big town, never was and probably never will be.  When I arrived home, the main street stretched only six blocks from one end to the other.  It was on this street the great folks from town held a colorful and quite stirring parade in my honor, and in honor of Henry Terry, when we returned from the war.

Before that, though, Henry and I stopped more

than twenty-five times on the trip from New York to California. We visited the homes of some of our fallen comrades, talked with parents and relatives, passed on anecdotes and tried in any way we could to soften the pain they were still suffering from the loss of their loved one. Henry Terry, who commanded the Group at Bassingbourn, was my close friend. I lived with him and his wife, Hazel, in England, and she hadn't yet arrived in the United States. Very obvious were the gold stars in the windows of the homes we visited on that sad but stirring trip to California. As we made these emotional stops it reminded me of some of the visits I'd made during my short furloughs before I returned to combat. Everywhere I stopped on that trip to visit families, they wanted me to take a bottle back to the boys in the squadron. When I returned to England, my luggage was packed to the brim with bottles of booze from home.

It was always my habit to stay in contact with the families of lost crewmen and friends from my squadron, at first with a letter then, if possible, with a visit. As a Second Lieutenant and bombardier of the B-17 Punchy, I was the only officer left and took up the task of writing to the families of those who went down. I tried to soften the unbearable, but I never really knew if I was succeeding.  I remember the letter I wrote to the family of our radio operator, Tech Sergeant Paul Payne, who died in Punchy when she went down.

"Dear Mrs. Payne and Family," I wrote.  "This heartbreaking news that I must send you promises to be one of the hardest jobs I have ever had to face.  I feel that you would appreciate hearing the details from somebody close to Paul.

"I am the bombardier on Paul's crew and during our training we grew to be great friends.  He was my favorite among the men as I, too, had spent the biggest part of my life beating about the country, and seldom came home unless I was hungry.  Your son died just as he lived, doing his job with complete disregard for danger.  Nothing ever seemed to bother him and I know he went the way he would have wanted to.  With him went our pilot..." and I proceeded to mention the other men, friends of the sergeant.

"They were on a very dangerous mission into France.  Payne was doing his part to make this a better world to live in. They had just left the English coast when another plane out of formation collided with their ship. Both ships exploded and fell into the Channel..." I said, trying my best to describe what happened.

I concluded the letter with, "All of his things have been packed by the boys and will be sent to you. His affairs are all in order, and I am taking steps to see that you receive the valuables that were left in the care of other crewmen.

"Please let me share a personal part of your sorrow, Mrs. Payne, for I feel a great deal of pain in losing a friend who had been more than near to me.

"With most sincere regrets and sympathies.

"I remain,

"Very truly yours,

"Lt. Charles S. Hudson."

Corny? Banal? Not enough?

Maybe. But the family didn't seem to think so, and that's what mattered.

Try it sometime. Write to a mother who has just lost her son. Use your most polished prose, and see how you do. I always did my best, for I believed in what I was writing.

During one furlough I visited in the hill country of McComas, West Virginia, far off the beaten path, to meet with the family and friends of my first pilot, Buck Edwards, who had been lost in action. The houses in the little village were built along a canyon-like wash, all in a row and held up by stilts on the steep slope to keep them above the water. These mountain folks felt very strongly about their boys in service, especially ones who had been killed in action. At each house along the way I had to re-tell the story of the courage of the man they all knew and loved, and how he had lived and died. At each house I had to have a swig or two of this very strong red wine they made locally. A few houses into the visit, talking about my fellow crewman, I became a really great bombardier because I became totally "bombed." Still, we had a wonderful, sad, moving time with laughter and tears, and good memories of a good man lost in the great war.

Speaking of gold stars, most of the stars in the windows of the homes of servicemen and women during the Second World War were blue. Many homes proudly displayed more than one blue star, some homes several. A blue star, indicating a family member in service, was replaced with a gold star if that person was killed, or missing in action. A few homes had more than one gold star in the window. The home of the five Sullivan brothers, boys who served together on the same ship in the United States Navy, displayed _five_ gold stars.

Times have changed and these things no longer seem as important as they once were, but in those days it

was not at all unusual to see folks choke up when they
passed the Sullivan house, or the house of a friend or
neighbor with a gold star in the window.  They remembered,
and missed the one represented by the gold star.

          Henry Terry and I couldn't accept bottles of
booze to carry back to the boys at Bassingbourn after these
New York to California visits.  The war was over.  We were
home for good.  In Taft, Mary and Terry and I choked up
when we pulled up in front of my old house.  My dear
mother, who was my friend and guardian all my life,
appeared on the porch steps as our parade of cars arrived.
The crowd with us fell silent as she came down the short
walk in front, smiling happily at me, reaching out for me.
She looked as though the cares of the world had dropped
from her shoulders.  There would be no gold star in her
window.  Her son was home, safe.  Most of us who have been
in combat and faced death fail to give enough credit to the
loved ones who faced every day not knowing.  Men and women
in hot combat are so busy dodging bullets and flak that
they usually thought only of the moment, of trying to stay
alive.  Those who remained at home, fathers and mothers and
wives and sons and daughters, and some husbands, could only
imagine what was happening, and pray, and dread the day the
telegram arrived, or the day they saw an officer or a high-

ranking enlisted man in a staff car pull up out in front.

They _knew_, in that instant, even before they really know.

My mother, eyes as misty as mine and Mary's, said, "I took your star down today, Charles, now let's go in the house and have some dinner."  Funny, but along with the pride they felt I suppose those back home might have in some way _hated_ those stars, or at least looked forward to the day they could remove them from the front window.

Mother is long gone now, and so is Mary, but I'll especially remember them on that day.  The war, the terrible pain, the death and destruction, all seemed suddenly many years before.  Flying combat missions and fearing enemy fighters and burning, tearing flak and dropping bombs were all in the past.  Friends I hadn't seen in years crowded around us, shouting and laughing and pounding me on the back and shaking my hand, and the hand of my friend and former commanding officer, Henry Terry. Everybody talked at once and I loved the sound in my ears. I loved them.

The merriment went on far into the night, then Orville Hall told me there was to be a big parade the next morning right down Center Street.  There were to be high school bands, dignitaries, and the whole town was going to turn out for the celebration.

"Tomorrow," Orville proudly said, "has been proclaimed to be <u>Charlie Hudson Day</u> in Taft!"

I knew it was Orville Hall's doing, my good friend Orville, much older than me and one who had been my mentor for years, as he was with his own sons. I remember Orville's teaching about how to recognize customers in the butcher shop so you could, as he required, always call them by their first name.

"Put little notes up on the cash register, Charlie. Notes like 'wide rear' or 'tall and skinny woman' or 'flat chest' then put their name on the same note with the reminder. That way, you can always remember them." I grinned to myself as I recalled sliding the old butcher cases open from the rear and leaning in over the meat so I could look out through the front glass of the case to see if the customer actually had a "wide rear" or not. I miss Orville Hall very much.

Mary and Henry Terry and I rode in one of two brightly decorated convertibles, the mayor and other town big shots rode in the other. Since the main street in Taft was only about six blocks long in those days, the whole parade went the entire distance to the end, then turned around and came all the way back again. Nobody, it seemed

to us, left their places at the curb, so we had the
opportunity to wave at many friends twice.

A real surprise was in store for us after the
parade, one that still chokes me up today.  It was a
surprise that would direct my life for the next several
years, one that would hold me in the area I loved and one
that, if I had not responded to a call for more adventure,
would to this day steer my life.

You have to remember that the Second World War
was the last of the great, stirring battles between "good"
and "evil."  There was a distinct group of bad guys in the
persons of Germany's Adolph Hitler and Italy's comical but
cruel Benito Mussolini, and Jap Emperor Hirohito, who never
had to face the terrible music whose overture he willingly
conducted.  Then there were some good guys.  The good guys
included President Franklin D. Roosevelt and Prime Minister
Winston Churchill and, yes, even Joseph Stalin from Russia.

The United States had been summarily and wickedly
attacked at Pearl Harbor on December 7, 1941, by the Empire
of Japan, by Hirohito and his side-kick, General Tojo, one
who <u>did</u> eventually pay the piper on the gallows.  Many of
our boys were killed.  Many innocent American civilians
were killed.  Many of our ships were sunk in the harbor.

Meanwhile, Hitler was systematically absorbing

most of Europe, and killing millions of Jews and others in the process.  He was a monster you could hate, and most of us did.  He was a point we could focus against, and when you threw in Italian dictator, Mussolini, we had some specific individuals who were out to hurt us, to destroy our country and our way of life, and enslave our people.

We had an ideology we were willing to resist, to fight, if necessary to <u>die</u>, to defeat.  We could not permit these people to take over our lives, and every citizen - that's <u>everyone</u>, including young children - understood. The kids collected pennies and the adults willingly gave dollars, and blood, and even their lives, to win the fight.

Most young men wanted to fight these devils to the death, and many, many did just that.  Germany and Italy quit, then Japan surrendered unconditionally on August 14, 1945, and the last of the great patriotic, civilian-supported wars ended.

Wars since then, including the "forgotten" Korean War, the generally scorned Viet Nam war, even "Desert Storm" and other more modern conflicts in the Middle East, lacked the popular support of the people, the overwhelming backing the citizens of the United States willingly offered to World War II.  Wars since WW II have appeared to be more political than patriotic, more involved with our image

overseas than whether or not an armed enemy planned to
occupy Washington and New York and Chicago and Los Angeles,
and enslave us and our children and our President.

In those days, before the surrender of Germany,
Italy and Japan, the war was everything. The war was the
prime topic of conversation; it was on everybody's lips and
in everybody's thoughts. Every newspaper headline screamed
of major victories, or defeats. Every life was directed at
winning the war. Songs were written and sung with vigor,
emotional songs and fighting songs and funny songs like
"We'll 'Heil' Right in Der Fuhrer's Face." We were
together. Soldiers on the street were honored.

Dramatic action motion pictures calling the hated
Germans "Krauts," and "Heinies," the Japanese "Japs" and
"cowardly little yellow bastards," the Italians "I-ties"
and other even less attractive nicknames, were made and
cheered by throngs. Actor John Wayne led us to victory in
"The Sands of Iwo Jima" and other battle pictures. Top
Hollywood actors fought on "Bataan" and "The Longest Day"
and "In Harm's Way" and many other battlegrounds in many
other popular motion pictures. Van Johnson and Henry Fonda
and James Cagney and James Garner and Cary Grant and
Gregory Peck and Clint Eastwood and Richard Burton and Lee
Marvin and Steve McQueen and Burt Lancaster and Charlton

Heston and many others fought on land, on the sea, in the air, and underwater in war films of the day, great action and drama films like "Mr. Roberts," "Up Periscope," "The Dirty Dozen," "Run Silent, Run Deep," "Operation Pacific," "Where Eagles Dare," "Midway," "Sink the Bismarck," and many, many more. In "Thirty Seconds Over Tokyo," the true story of the dangerous and B-25 raid on Japan by General James Doolittle's gallant squadron of flyers, several major actors including Spencer Tracy helped Americans feel a little better about Pearl Harbor. Tracy, playing Doolittle, led the raid that bombed Jap cities and made Jap soldiers, who later executed some of our young flyers as "war criminals," appear as the sadistic monsters we knew they were.

No sacrifice was too great in those days. This is difficult to believe now, especially by younger people who feel differently about our country and other countries, and who are more reluctant about fighting and killing for a patriotic cause. Many younger people today do not understand when they see an elderly veteran with tears in his eyes, his hand firmly over his heart, as Old Glory passes in a parade. Many think it is too sentimental, even foolish. They cannot grasp, except, perhaps, at "The Wall" in Washington, what it means to willingly fight and die for one's country.

Many make fun of it now, perhaps with at least
some reason, but back then it truly was "America, right or
wrong." Didn't we all know that America was right? Of
course we did. Most youngsters will never understand the
emotion felt by those still living veterans of WWII and
Korea, and even a few their own age from Viet Nam, who
choke up or weep at the sound of "taps." These young
people are missing one of the deepest emotions a human can
feel, a great love for one's country, a love that will
allow discussion and even disagreement, but a love that
remains at the bottom line, whatever else happens.

I feel sorry for them.

Things were different in Taft, California, in
1945. Back then, what was about to happen to Mary and me
was not all that unusual, though it didn't happen every day
either. All over the country, returning veterans were
special, and honored. We'd won the great war, and nothing
was too good for us. Those of us who lived through the war
were proud of the victory, and what we'd done to bring it
about, and that pride was nourished and shared by the folks
who stayed home and helped the war effort in their own way.

Things will never be that way again, and perhaps
that's good. War is never a good solution, and pride in

killing may not, after all, be noble.  Korean vets came home and people asked "Where have you been?"  Nothing had changed much, and they hadn't really been missed except by loved ones.  Even many of the loved ones had little idea that American men and women were dying in great numbers in that mediocre and relatively unimportant little country in the cold Far East.

Viet Nam vets snuck home, hoping nobody would notice, though they certainly didn't like it, nor did they have any reason to be anything but proud.

So it might be difficult to comprehend, but at the end of the parade in Taft that homecoming day the whole group drove to another street downtown and pulled up in front of a very nice bar.  We, Terry and I, thought it was just another place to grab a drink in celebration.  Mary was grinning a secretive smile.  We piled out of our cars, but Orville, who had arranged the whole thing, ran ahead, pulled out a key, and opened the door.

Congenial, I thought.  My friends had probably reserved the bar for us, and I planned to have two or three drinks instead of just one.  It really was nice.

Then Orville, with the biggest smile on his face you can imagine, hurried back to the car.  Handing me the key and some other papers, he said, "Charlie, it's _yours_, from the people of Taft, for what you did in the war."

The papers were paid up mortgages on the bar. It was free and clear. It was mine.

I looked at Mary, then at Henry, then at my crowd of friends, and a lump formed in my throat. My eyes filled with tears, and so what if they did? These people had touched me very deeply with their wonderful gift. A bar was what I wanted when I came back from the war, and they had arranged for my dream to come true. How do you figure friends like that?

I was overwhelmed, and if I wept, so did Mary and Henry and Orville and many of the others. The thing was, I never figured they owed me anything. I wanted their friendship, and I was honored with the parties and the parade, but I never expected more than that. Yes, I was overwhelmed.

From a butcher to a rough-edged oil field worker to a decorated soldier to a bar owner, I was in business in Taft, and I made the best of it. Adventure called from time to time, but I managed to dull that edge by sharpening my golf game. The bar, which turned into two bars, then three bars, and finally four bars in surrounding cities, did very well. Each was called "Buckhorn Bar," and folks took to them. At each bar I opened a driving range and putting green and these facilities also made handsome profits.  Not only had I regained my amateur status with the Professional Golfers Association, but as my game came together and my bank account increased, I went on the tour as an amateur in 1953.

This was the same PGA who would, in a few years, suspend me without a real hearing because I appeared to be in serious trouble with the law.  But that was later on.  I was touring and enjoying the play.

A mistake?  Who can say?  I loved, and still love, the game of golf.  Even today I give frequent lessons to celebrities and to regular players who want to improve their game.  You have to be a golfer to understand the love you develop for the game.  Non-golfers, and there are a few left in the world, think that hitting a little white ball around a big field, trying to knock it into tiny holes in the ground, is silly.  But then when they try the game of golf themselves, many quickly become converted and are often the most vociferous in their praise of this marvelous game.

The problem with the tour back in the fifties was that the top prize might stretch to seventy five hundred or so, with the winner getting maybe two or three thousand dollars.  These were not the days of the million dollar pro games currently on television. The top stars of the game were celebrities within the golf circle, but they weren't that well-known outside the game. Winners would often end up lending money from their purse to losers, knowing that it would come back next game when the winners lost and the losers won. It was a wonderful time of friendship and competition, but the game wasn't paying me much.

Meanwhile, back home, my bars were beginning to fail. Some of my employees were stealing from me, and customers wanted me there, not in some city far away playing golf. A local bar is a personal business, and if the owner isn't there, patrons drift away. If Sam Malone, of television's "Cheers," didn't spend much of his time behind the bar, the place wouldn't be nearly so successful. Elray Lumpkin, my manager and one of the few honest bartenders I know, did all he could to keep the operation a success. For awhile he succeeded, but the business needed the owner to be on site and I wasn't. Speaking of honest employees, Jack Foster ran another of my operations, and although he had a dream, he was also very honest with me. Jack wanted to be a singer, and he always said so. But he couldn't sing. He also wanted to be a talent agent, a person who places. singers and bands into nightclubs and bars. Jack, I'm happy to report, is currently living in Lake Tahoe, and working as a talent agent.

       Bucky Metcalf came into my life about the time I
was selling my bars.  I wasn't hurting at all.  I didn't
"need a job" as the old saying goes, but I will admit that
I missed the action I'd become accustomed to in the Army,
then on the golf tour.  When Metcalf called, I heard in the
distance the siren sound of adventure.  What did he want?
His request was simple enough.

       "There's an old Vultee V1A in Costa Rica.  It's
the exact airplane needed for a Warner Brothers motion
picture being filmed on the life of band leader Harry
Richmond," Metcalf explained.  "Richmond co-piloted this
airplane on a transoceanic flight to Paris, and the studio
wants to use the original plane in the movie."

       The airplane the movie people wanted was not only
the very one Richmond had flown, but it was one of only
very few V1A's ever built by Vultee.  The one in Costa
Rica, an airplane with a distinguished history in other
ways as well, was suspected to be the very last one in
existence.  It had not been an easy airplane to locate,
explained Bucky Metcalf, but the movie company, with
Metcalf doing the searching, had finally found it in San
Jose.

       "We need an experienced pilot to go down and

check it out, then fly it home. The pay will be excellent, and there's no limit on the expense account. Would you be interested, Charlie?" asked Metcalf.

I was a pilot looking for some exciting work. Maybe I should have, but not knowing, I didn't hang up on Bucky. This seemed my kind of job.

Excitement!

Adventure in a foreign land!

A substantial paycheck and all expenses from a movie company that could, according to Bucky, lead to more paychecks from other movie companies!

Mary and I said farewell, but only for what we were certain was a short time. Going down, checking out the airplane, then flying it home to California should have been easy. My flight to San Jose was smooth, and my drive to the nearby location of the V1A was the same. I thought about the conversation with Mary just before I left. We figured that even if the plane had one or two problems that had to be handled before the long flight, the flying part of the job should be routine.

Problems? I couldn't believe my eyes. The antiquated old V1A was a pile of <u>junk</u>. Once a luxury airplane for the very rich and famous, it had been setting on that hot, wet, jungle-land airstrip for <u>years</u>. Up on blocks, with poles supporting the wings and fuselage, it was probably the saddest spectacle of a flying machine I'd ever seen. Sweating in the humid jungle heat, I studied the situation. Every single external antenna had long since been broken off, and the wings, which couldn't be stolen without tools, were full of holes, probably ripped in by frustrated thieves. The sad old airplane was infected with wing well rot, and many of her control cables were gone or very deficient.

Inside, the airplane was <u>rancid</u>. The passenger seats were corroded and rotting. All the metal sheeting was decayed or stripped away, and every instrument but two had long since been cannibalized. At the time, the two remaining instruments seemed to stare up at me like a sad basset hound looking for its master. The pilot's seat had rusted away and the wooden stool I was sitting on nearly tipped over backwards as I deliberated.

How can I best describe this "airplane" from my past? If I reach for words, if I really try to sum it up, if I meditate and contemplate and ponder, only one descriptive word comes to mind.

This airplane was <u>garbage</u>!

But wait a minute!

Hold on just a minute.

Garbage? Yes. Trash? Perhaps. Debris? Maybe.
But <u>not</u> a <u>total loss</u>. This tired old airplane, I knew in
my heart, still had a possibility or two. It was junk,
without a doubt, but there was a faint spark of life
somewhere in its rusted and torn parts and sagging wings.
I could feel it in my bones. This ancient airplane, once
on the cutting edge of aviation technology, could be a real
adventure in restoration. It could be a genuine challenge.
Parts and repairs were probably still available in Los
Angeles, and there was, oddly enough, an excellent repair
facility on Costa Rica with top notch mechanics to help me.
Meanwhile, money didn't seem to be a problem.

Why not? It might take more than the few days
originally anticipated, but then and there, hot and wet and
with more than a little apprehension, the decision was
made. I would save this once noble airplane, this airplane
that had flown some of the most famous people in the world.
She would rise from the ignominious junk heap and the
devouring jungle. I would give her a new life, and fly her
into motion picture fame and history back to California.

Sooner or later, that is.

She didn't have to be perfect, she just had to
fly home. Yes, I could do that, with the help of SAYA
Aviation, the American-owned aircraft repair facility in

San Jose.  The country had sent many of its young men to Los Angeles to learn various specialties in aircraft repair, and they had become quite good at their jobs.  The airport had airplanes from many countries lined up awaiting repair.  They towed the old airplane carefully into a hangar, and went to work on her under my direction.  We replaced the wing rot sections and every other weakness we could find.  There were no manuals on the aircraft, so I checked myself out on her while she was jacked up.

What SAYA didn't have was a "test pilot," so, naturally, I volunteered.  While they were working on the V1A, they paid me five hundred dollars for each "engineering test flight" I made in one of the other airplanes they were repairing.  Since I was checked out in most types of airplanes, this worked very well for me, with some time on my hands, and for them.  It worked out to about one test flight a week.

During the "restoration," which eventually took four long, hot, muggy months, I stayed in the Pan American Hotel in San Jose.  It was there that I met Vic Stadter, another pilot from the United States.  My life was becoming a plot, and with Vic, the plot thickened.  Of course I had no idea then, but Vic Stadter would lead me into one of the greatest adventures in my life, an adventure that would

eventually be made into a motion picture starring Charles
Bronson.  Before that, though, Vic would lead me into a
business from which I made a great deal of money.  Vic was
in Costa Rica on what he insisted was the hottest deal of
the century.  It was a can't-miss, get-rich-quick scheme.

"Charlie," said Vic with great enthusiasm after
we got to know each other, "I'm raking in real big bucks.
I mean, _real_ big bucks!"

"OK," I answered, "I'm interested.  Are you
robbing banks?"

Vic laughed.  "No, this is almost entirely legal,
and _you_ can get _in_ on it, too."

I've never turned my back on a relatively legal
way to make a profit. "What do I have to do, Vic?" I asked.

He looked around carefully, but nobody in the bar
was paying any attention.  "Are you ready for this,
Charlie? All you have to do is load an airplane with exotic
animals from down here, and then fly them up _there_.  That's
_it_.  People are there to unload them and haul them away,
and you make a real chunk of money on each flight."

"Flying exotic animals?" I asked.  "That's _it_?"

"That's it, pal.  You know, birds and monkeys and
snakes and tapirs and stuff.  It's _easy_."

"Birds and monkeys and snakes and tapirs?  Tell

me, Vic, what the hell is a <u>tapir</u>?  And who <u>feeds</u> these
things until they're picked up?

        "Well, naturally, <u>you</u> do, but only until you get
them back to the states, then somebody else takes over.
They hand you your money, unload the animals, and that's
it."

        I must admit I had misgivings, but on the whole
the idea didn't sound too shabby.  The wheels were turning
in my head.

        "Give it some thought," Vic Stadter enthused,
"and in the meantime, I'll help you put together that heap
of a Vultee you're working on."

        Vic did seem to be raking in big money as an
animal hauler.  We discussed the matter further as he and I
helped direct the work on the old airplane.  Flying exotic
animals from Costa Rica and other Central and South
American countries to pet store outlets in the United
States was, according to Vic, a veritable gold mine.  He
insisted I was missing a wonderful opportunity by not
jumping on the gravy train.  I've never been one to
intentionally miss any gravy train passing nearby, so I
continued to consider the idea.

        Meanwhile, we finally "finished" the plane and
tested her in the air.  One cowling did rip off and we had

to wait two more weeks for SAYA to make another, but the
fact that I'm writing this book proves that the airplane
did fly.  From its original appearance any logical person
would have thought it was less than one step from the junk
yard.

In fact, the V1A flew <u>great</u>.

With Vic Stadter's encouragement and help I just
naturally loaded the old plane with exotic animals before
taking off for the United States.  Might as well kill two
birds with one stone, I decided, you'll pardon the
expression.

## Chapter Ten   The Great White Animal Hauler

Our Vultee V1A, with many holes in the instrument
panel but otherwise almost sleek again, was a great
airplane for its day.  It was a flying machine truly before
its time. Accepted and expected now, the Vultee had
engineering features that were marvels bsck then.  It had
retractable landing gears if you could figure out how to
work them, hydraulic flaps that did also happen to be tied
into the landing gear system, and a single stage
supercharger that usually worked great if you waited until
the airplane was at ten thousand feet.

I had a chance to test that latter engineering
theory sooner than I wanted.  I learned that if you're
facing a mountain dead ahead, you <u>can</u> kick in the Vultee's
supercharger at only a few <u>hundred</u> feet of altitude.  I
learned that it helps even though the engineers said it
wouldn't.  You <u>do</u> get an extra surge of power to climb out,
and you get it right <u>now</u>.

The Vultee V1A I was getting ready to take off
that day in Costa Rica had a very distinguished career
before Bucky Metcalf discovered her on the jungle airstrip.
If her fuselage could only have talked, what a story it
would have told.  Lining up to take off, listening to her

throbbing Wright Cyclone engine, I considered the past of
the gallant Vultee.  In her younger days, that very
airplane had set a speed record of 192 miles per hour
between Los Angeles and San Francisco.

And much, much more.

Only seven V1A's were completed by Vultee before
Boeing came up with a twin-engined model that competed well
enough to stop the Vultee production line.  On the Vultee
line at that time were a few unfinished V1A's.  The
airplanes that were finished by Vultee flew passengers for
Western Airlines between Los Angeles, Riverside, San Diego,
and Long Beach.

William Randolph Hearst, the rich and famous
newspaper publisher, bought two of the new V1A's from
Vultee and had them converted into luxury airplanes for a
very specific job.  He insisted on flush riveting, a 12
cylinder Wright Cyclone engine for extra speed and safety,
and he paid designers to create fancy interiors.  These two
airplanes were used by actress Marian Davies to fly back
and forth between Hollywood and Hearst's home in San
Simeon, California, now a state park known as "Hearst
Castle."  Each plane had a well paid pilot who simply stood
by for her convenience.

One of the fancy and very expensive Hearst V1A's

was wrecked on the San Simeon airstrip, but Davies was not
involved.  Eventually, Hearst gave the other V1A to the
Chicago Tribune where it was to be used for a special
around the world flight.  The pilot's name was Frank
Merrill and the co-pilot was famous band leader Harry
Richmond.  In those days, you didn't just fly across the
ocean and around the world at the drop of a hat. Such a
long flight was still a very big deal, especially with a
co-pilot as famous as Richmond, during a time when big band
leaders were major celebrities.

On the initial leg of the around the world
flight, across the Atlantic Ocean to Paris, yet another
"engineering marvel" was installed.  Thousands and
thousands of ping-pong balls were put into each wing, and
into every other compartment and cavity in the airplane.
Engineers figured that if the plane did go down in the
ocean, it certainly couldn't sink with all those air-filled
balls aboard.  The V1A didn't go down, and when she was
finally unloaded in Los Angeles after the round the world
flight, the Hearst people recovered their investment by
selling nearly ten million dollars worth of ping pong balls
as souvenirs of the highly publicized adventure.  It was
like space flight today.  Wouldn't <u>you</u> give a dollar or two
for a souvenir that had gone to the moon or to Mars and

back?  Well, I would.  Some of those famous ping pong balls
are still around.

The only problem with the original plan was, the
writers who were in the early planning stages of a motion
picture on Harry Richmond didn't figure on the band
leader's initial reaction.  He wanted no more of flying a
V1A over the ocean or anywhere else.  The first leg across
the Atlantic had cooled his ardor for the whole globe-
circling flight.  Richmond dropped out of the plan and
Merrill went on with another co-pilot.  If the motion
picture was to be made, it would have to say that Richmond
didn't enjoy long flights with ping pong balls as flotation
devices in case of ditching.  The band leader came home on
a boat, and the airplane once used to fly Marian Davies
from Hollywood to luxurious Hearst Castle, into the waiting
arms of William Randolph Hearst (though anybody who has
taken the "upper" tour of the famous castle has seen the
Hearst and Davies "separate bedrooms"), flew on around the
world.

Back in Chicago, the Tribune then gave the plane
to a very famous early day pilot by the name of Jimmy
Angel, a soldier of fortune, gold prospector and general
adventurer.  Angel's Falls in Venezuela, where Angel took
the plane, are named after this famous aviation pioneer.

The restored V1A I was taxiing to the end of the runway to take off for the United States was eventually picked up in New Guinea, flown to Costa Rica, and there it seemed to have ended its distinguished life, rusting away and no longer in the limelight.

Until Bucky Metcalf located her, and Charlie Hudson and friends restored her.

"Stop, Senor, _stop_!"

The shouting broke into my reverie. I've always loved airplanes, and this one was very special, indeed. I looked out the pilot's window and saw a jeep that had pulled up and was speeding alongside us, parallel to the taxiway. The police/soldiers/local-extortion-squad was waving wildly at me to shut down the engine. The officer in charge was standing in the front seat, holding on to the top of the windshield with one hand and slashing one finger of his other hand across his throat to indicate to me, I guessed, that he wanted the engine stopped. Or that he was thinking of committing suicide with a sharp knife, but I knew what he wanted.

One of the troubles with the Vultee V1A was her hot-start characteristics. Cold start, too, for that matter, but once warmed up, it was best to keep a V1A going. If she was shut down, she would balk at re-starting

because her battery would never come up to strength. A
booster was needed, and had to be brought to the plane.
Once in the air, of course, she used a magneto. Shutting
down the engine if only for a moment or two could become a
complex matter.

"_Senor!_  Please _stop!_" the one in charge shouted.
I couldn't hear him, but I could read his lips, and his
suicidal gesture across his throat.

There was no doubt in my mind what they wanted.
They knew I'd loaded the plane with animals.  In fact, at
that very moment a young tapir was wandering up and down
the aisle, unafraid and generally curious about the inside
of the airplane.  The snakes were in burlap bags, but the
newly vaccinated, white-faced capuchin monkeys, unhappy to
the last one, were angrily chattering and screaming from
inside their temporary cages.  This somewhat unnerving
cacophony of strident sound was tolerable for the hours it
would take to get home because the monkeys had cost two
bucks each and were worth about twenty-two each in the
States, at wholesale.  All things considered, what I wanted
most was to take off as quickly as possible and head for
_home_.  What the squad on the ground wanted was their
tribute, their "port tax," their pay-off to allow me to fly
away.  It wasn't legal, but they did have real guns.

I've never cared for that sort of thing. It wasn't right and it wasn't fair. Besides, I didn't have any money. I'd been living on Warner Brother's credit, and now I was on my own. My new friend and passenger, a woman I called "Jungle Judy," didn't have any cash either. Another American I met at the hotel, Judy had persuaded me to fly her home for that very reason, no money to buy an airline ticket.

Waving brightly to them, smiling down at them all the time, I shouted, "Goodbye, my friends. I've enjoyed your beautiful country." I waved some more. "I'm sorry, but I must go now." Without asking Judy, a pretty woman who said she was a scientist studying monkeys in Costa Rica, I eased the throttle forward toward the perforated instrument panel. The old V1A lurched forward against her brakes.

"No, no, no!" they shouted from their jeep. "You must stop the engine!"

"Bye-bye," I responded with a happy wave as I released the brakes. I had to turn the ship around and line up. Meanwhile, they merely cruised alongside, slowly drawing in front of me, waving all the time. When it became obvious to them that I was going to take off, they rushed on ahead and then swerved the jeep directly out into

the middle of the runway, facing me.  By then I had already
started my take-off run.  The old V1A thundered and surged
forward, gaining speed.  I was certain they would pull off
the runway once they realized their extortion plot had
failed, though at that moment we could see them all
standing in the jeep, still wildly waving at me to stop.
In the next few seconds, three hard facts became evident.

One, they were <u>not</u> going to pull off the runway.

Two, I didn't have nearly enough speed to take
off <u>over</u> them.

And, three, I was going <u>much</u> too fast to stop.

Since back in my Taft days, back when I was
washing down airplanes for stick time, I'd worked hard at
becoming a good pilot. Although in the military, as a
bombardier, I never questioned what my pilot was doing, I
knew that I was a damned good pilot myself. I felt the
power in the big wheel of the V1A and I heard the strong
song of her mighty engine.  Yes, although I wasn't going
nearly fast enough to take off cleanly, what I planned
could be done.

Hurtling faster and faster toward the parked jeep
full of waving men, I hauled quickly back on the wheel.
The V1A seemed surprised at my move, but she responded.
She struggled momentarily then wallowed into the air a few

feet. She knew as well as I that she wasn't going fast enough to take off and fly.

So did Jungle Judy, in the co-pilot's seat, wide-eyed in terror and certainly at that instant wishing with all her heart that she had done something, _anything_, to raise enough money for a commercial flight home.

We cleared the heads of the wildly ducking men by inches then, as I knew she would, the V1A settled back on the runway with a hard thud. Her landing gears strained, her tires screamed, she bounced raggedly once, twice, then she settled smoothly back into her take off run. Before the maneuver I'd noted that we had enough runway, if I could clear the jeep.

The old William Randolph Hearst airplane lifted grandly and steadily off, her pilot, her co-pilot, and possibly even her load of exotic animals all breathing a great sigh of relief. The tapir in the aisle, however, appeared totally unconcerned. Behind and below, the frustrated con-men could only watch as we disappeared into the sunset.

We landed first at Tehuantepec, Mexico, where I had a chance to figure out fuel and oil consumption and other data. No problems. The V1A was flying very well, and consumption figures were within specifications. We added fuel and went on to Acapulco, where we spent the night.

Unfortunately, the ceiling was down the next morning, and it was raining. With the tapir still running up and down the aisle, we took off into the rain and mist, heading for Los Angeles. Along the floor of the Vultee V1A, from front to rear, was a long square box through which the control cables were routed. Some of the monkeys had worked their way out of their cages and gained access to this box, but we figured they were just as safe in there as anywhere else. The V1A fuselage is open inside all the way from the nose to the very tip of the tail, so the monkeys were naturally in these areas as well, from one end of the airplane to the other. The cages, built as temporary housing, weren't really all that secure.

The rain, meanwhile, was coming through leaks around the windows in the old fuselage and soaking us both, so my friend, Jungle Judy, was stretching about the cockpit, jamming pieces of Kleenex into the holes to try to stop the leaks. I was maintaining an altitude of little more than a couple of hundred feet or so in order to see the ocean below, but the rain was making it very difficult.

We were about one mile off the coast when Judy screamed.

"Look out!!"

Ahead and rushing toward us through the mist was a _mountain_! It was on an island I hadn't seen on any charts. Reacting instinctively, I stood the Vultee on one wing and pulled back on the wheel, putting us into a high speed stall. The V1A started to sink on me, so I reached over and shoved the supercharger wide open. Even though it wasn't supposed to be used until the plane reached an altitude of ten thousand feet, the engine got just enough extra boost to pull out of the stall and continue our one hundred eighty degree turn.

Shaken but still confident, I returned to our base course. But the damage had been done. Those cages not yet breached by their occupants were tossed about in the back by the violent maneuver of the airplane. Frightened capuchin monkeys were all over the place. Each one seemed to be angrier than the last one, and each was trying to find a safe place to hide, not knowing that there _wasn't_ a safe place in the whole damned airplane. Only the snakes were still in their bags, but the bags were scattered all over the floor and almost certainly some of them would soon escape. Vic Stadter hadn't said it would be _anything_ like that.

We had monkeys in the tail, monkeys in the nose, and monkeys in the control cable box. We had a thick-skinned baby tapir still wandering up and down the aisle, apparently too dumb to be afraid and probably enjoying the ride. Several monkeys had crawled into the nose, and while I continued to fight the rain and try to see what was ahead in the mist, some of them found they could watch me through the holes in the instrument panel where gauges were once mounted. This seemed to calm them.

I flew on, the trusting little white faces of several monkeys staring up at me through the instrument panel with complete confidence.

Heading for Los Angeles Airport, we passed over Chino, California, where I knew a repair facility was located. We flew on, but within the next ten minutes or so, red lights began to flash on the instrument panel.

"What's wrong, Charlie?" asked Judy.

"I'm not certain in this airplane," I answered. "We could be running out of fuel, or there could be something else wrong."

"What are you going to do?"

"Rather than take a chance, I think we should go back to Chino to land," I said with confidence, turning the plane back the other way. We sighted Chino, and I flipped the switch to lower the landing gears. Naturally, as I should have suspected, nothing happened. The monkeys

didn't worry, though. They continued to watch me through
the instrument panel with real interest, as carefully as
only a curious monkey can watch anything.

The Vultee V1A had a unique landing gear/flap
mechanism. It was designed well enough, but you had to
keep your mind on what you were doing. Picture it this
way. There was one control motor with a gear case and
shift lever to handle both functions. When you were using
the motor, you shifted the lever into the retractable
landing gear mode to raise or lower the landing gear. Then
you shifted into flap position to work the flaps. Simple
enough? Yes, but it got more complicated.

If you were _not_ using the motor, that is, if the
motor or a circuit failed and you had to use the hand-crank
to move the gear or the flaps, everything worked _opposite_.
To raise the gear by hand crank, you moved the gear shift
lever to the _flap_ position, not the landing gear position.
To work the flaps by hand crank, you had to put the gear
shift lever into the _landing gear_ position. Why? I have
no idea. Flaps and gears are normally worked about the
same time, during take offs and landings, but I guess the
engineers figured that the motor would never fail, and if
it did fail the pilot would be skilled enough to handle the
situation.

I never figured I'd have to use this idiosyncratic system, so I wasn't too worried, but suddenly the motor had failed and we were in no position to get out an operator's manual, even if one existed. Desperately trying to remember the settings and the sequences, we got ready to crank the gear down by hand. This should have been no real problem once I recalled where to set the gear shift lever.

There was, however, one minor problem. In order to get to the crank, which was mounted in a compartment near my right leg, I had to move the leg out of the way. This was the leg whose foot was controlling the right rudder, something the engineers hadn't considered and probably the reason why one of William Randolph Hearst's two expensive airplanes crashed on the San Simeon airstrip.

With Judy's right foot controlling the right rudder from her co-pilot position, and my left foot controlling the left rudder, I began to crank the landing wheels down as rapidly as I could manage, banging both our legs in the process. Shifting the wheel/flap gear lever quickly, I cranked down the flaps, then shifted back to the landing gear. We were on final approach, I was still cranking, and Judy and I were still trying to coordinate two separate legs into reasonably logical rudder movements.

Olney 248

        As we swept over the end of the runway and flared
out to land, we ran out of gas.  What happened was, when
the airplane tilted with its tail down and its nose up, we
were so low on fuel that any gas remaining in the tank
flowed back away from the fuel pickup. I was still
frantically cranking down the landing gear with one hand
and controlling the ailerons with the other when we touched
down.

        In fact, the gear didn't come all the way down,
but it was down far enough to support the plane in spite of
the hard landing that shook loose any remaining cages, and
released any remaining monkeys.  There's nothing like the
sound of an angry, frightened capuchin monkey.  It's a
screaming howl the little bastards make, far louder than
you would think such a small animal could emit.  With the
mighty Wright Cyclone engine by then silent. the din was
terrific.

        But we made it, and if I do say so, it was a
magnificent landing under the circumstances.  The monkeys
peering at me through the holes in the instrument panel,
cute little creatures who had no idea how close they had
come to going to monkey heaven, seemed to be staring up at
me with new respect.  We coasted to a stop on the runway,
and as the instrument panel monkeys disappeared to examine

this new stationary situation and these new sounds from
their recently released friends, both Judy and I breathed a
great sigh of relief.

Fate wasn't finished with me yet. Learning the
rules of my new business of animal hauling had only just
begun, and I was about to be taught yet another lesson.
Outside, some airport workers had pulled up to the plane.
Hoping to help, they were preparing to open the door to see
what was wrong. My voice literally caught in my throat.

They _couldn't_ do _that_!

"NO! DON'T OPEN THE DOOR!!" I shouted back at
them.

Too late.

They were there to help. They were worried about
me. They opened the door of the Vultee V1A right there on
the runway of the Chino airport.

One thing is for sure. If those line workers are
still there today, all these years later, I'm absolutely
certain they have never since opened an airplane door
without first asking. Instantly monkeys, birds, tapirs and
other creatures hurtled out the door and scattered in every
direction. The airport workers, terrified at that moment,
tumbled backwards in frightened astonishment. Nothing like
that had ever happened to them before.

The monkeys and other creatures?

All they wanted was to get as far from Charlie Hudson and his airplane as they possibly could. They had recognized the airplane's open door as their opportunity for a mass escape, and they had seized it. They were all over the place, running down the runway and heading across the field, alone and in pairs and in groups. Some of the exotic birds were long gone and a few of the snakes were slithering about in confusion, probably hoping to find their bags again.

Did that end my problems? After all, I had returned the plane to the United States, and I did have a good fee coming from Warner Brothers.

No, it did _not_ end my problems.

"I had to land," I explained when they all calmed down. "I'm out of gas," I said.

"That's OK," answered the guy who opened the door. "We'll get you towed back to the hangar. But what about all these animals?"

"Well, I guess we'll have to catch them," I said with a confidence I didn't really feel. For the next two or three hours we caught animals and brought them back to their jury-rigged cages. That part did seem to work out. I didn't have any money for fuel or anything else, but I

did have a plane load of animals. They were legal and I
owned them. The word spread and soon it seemed everybody
in Chino was at the airport, chasing the few remaining
animals. One by one they brought them back and then the
idea struck me. If you've been out there on the front
lines, chasing a wild animal across an airport, and you
finally catch it, and it doesn't bite off your finger, you
can get kind of attached to the little sonofabitch. A kind
of a bonding occurs.

      "I'll tell you what I'll do," I said to the next
one to bring in a live monkey. "I'll sell that monkey to
you for only twenty dollars, but you have to get it out of
here before the people come to examine my load. And that
price goes for all the others in cages, too."

      The first guy looked at the cute little monkey,
by then nestling in his arms. "You have a deal," he said,
peeling off a twenty and handing it to me. At that moment
I realized that I could get out of the mess I was in.

      Before long I'd sold several of the monkeys at
twenty dollars each. When the import people came to
inspect my load, they hit me with another bill for three
hundred bucks, but by then Bucky Metcalf had arrived and he
took over the expenses. With fuel in the airplane, I flew
to Whiteman Airpark in the San Fernando Valley north of Los

Angeles and parked the ship until the next morning, when
the pilots from Warner Brothers arrived. It took only a
short taxi to the end of the runway for them to say they
wouldn't touch the old Vultee for any amount of money, and
they insisted their decision had nothing to do with the
strong smell of animal dung in the fuselage.

"There's no <u>way</u> I'm going to fly this airplane,"
said one of the Warner pilots, even after I explained that
I had flown it all the way from Costa Rica. You can still
see the plane today, though. It was eventually used in a
movie called "Untarnished Angels" with Rock Hudson and Lana
Turner. I went back and served as pilot during the movie,
probably because I was the only one not afraid of the old
airplane.

Eventually the plane wound up in New Mexico,
where a pilot spent a ton of money to restore and refurbish
it. He flew it around the country, seeking the true
history of the plane. That's how I met him, and I couldn't
believe what the old Vultee had become. She was beautiful,
almost brand new.

In a way, I was glad, but in another way, I
didn't really care. I was hauling exotic animals full time
by then, in a brand new airplane, and making a bundle doing
it, too. This was all before I got into some very serious

trouble with the law.  That was coming.

Meanwhile, the newspaper headlines in Riverside, California, caught my attention one day.

WOMAN SUES NEIGHBOR FOR ASSAULT AND BATTERY

MONKEY CAPER PARTS NEIGHBORS

DEAD ANIMAL ASSAULT IS LAW BREAKER

For years I kept my mouth shut about something that happened, something I watched very carefully in the newspapers.  I knew what the problem was in Riverside, but I don't know if the lawyers ever figured it out.  It had to do with something that happened near the end of my first animal hauling trip in the old Vultee.  One thing Vic Stadter had been very emphatic about.

"Charlie, don't ever land with any dead animals aboard," he advised.  "The import people will immediately quarantine your whole load, and you'll be wandering around in paperwork forever.  Just be sure that all of them are alive and looking very healthy when you get inspected after landing."

With this advice in mind, Judy had gone to the rear to check the monkeys as we were approaching Los Angeles across the desert from the east.  Sure enough, a handful of them had departed this life for one reason or another.  Some of them had been fighting, and some of them

were just frightened even though we tried to treat them
well.  I hated to see the cute little things passing away
on my airplane, but my sincere feelings of regret didn't
make the problem go away.  Vic had said no dead animals,
and I had dead monkeys aboard with the airport only a few
more minutes away.

I gave Judy her instructions.  "Bring the poor
little things up to me one by one, and I'll take care of
them."

She did.  She brought the little dead monkeys to
the flight deck and I tossed them out the pilot's window.
They couldn't be hurt any more than they already were, and
it would solve my immediate problem.  I felt sure we
weren't yet over any populated area, though down below
there were  small housing developments scattered about east
of Riverside.  There was no way I could hit any of them, I
was certain.  Wasn't I once the lead bombardier of the
Eighth Air Force?  Who would know better than me, even if I
was dropping dead monkeys instead of live bombs?

When we landed, every animal on board was alive
and healthy, ready to make a run for it if the door was
ever opened.

That didn't end the story.  A few days later,
Bucky Metcalf was chuckling when he showed me the newspaper

article.  Even he didn't know the truth, though he may have
suspected.  This woman in Riverside, east of Los Angeles,
had been standing in her back yard when a dead monkey came
flying in. She naturally thought it was her next door
neighbor, a real low life, who had thrown the poor little
thing over the fence, so she stormed around and rang her
neighbor's front door bell.  When the neighbor lady
answered, she hit the completely astonished woman in the
face with the dead monkey.

     Two lawsuits resulted.  One, for assault and
battery, and the other for throwing a dead animal at a
living person.

     I remained to this day, until you read this, as
the only one who knew what really happened.

## Chapter Eleven   The REAL Animal Hauler

The sturdy twin-engined Douglas DC-3, known as a
"C-47" or "Gooney Bird" in the United States Air Force and
by other names in other military and civilian capacities,
was an extraordinary airplane.  Stodgy, solid, rather
unglamorous, the DC-3 was as reliable as any airplane ever
built.  She had, for her day, a cavernous cargo hold, good
range and relative comfort.  As a fighting military
airplane and as a passenger-hauling civilian, the husky DC-
3 compiled a record of dependability that will never be
equaled.  If the B-17 Flying Fortress, all bristling with
guns and plated with armor, was the single most glamorous
bomber ever built, then the C-47 was the consummate plain-

Olney 257

Jane transporter of wartime troops and supplies. Or, in prettier civilian clothing and with soft seats, airline passengers.

Not many know it, but in her military role the DC-3 also flew combat, especially during the Korean War. C-47's often labored back to K-16 or some other battered, freezing-cold airstrip in "the land of the morning calm" shattered and broken. From leaflet, loudspeaker and spy-drop missions, C-47's would struggle home with ailerons and other parts dangling and flapping in the wind, having been directly hit again and again by Chinese and to a lesser extent North Korean anti-aircraft fire. A skilled combat pilot could fly the faithful C-47 by her trim tabs if her main control surfaces were shot up and malfunctioning. Many C-47's landed with flat tires, great holes in the fuselage and tail, and one of her two engines sputtering or stopped altogether. She was a slow airplane, and under the very low altitude mission conditions of the Korean war, fairly easy to hit. But the C-47 was tough, and although some were lost, she was very difficult to shoot down.

A pleasure to fly, the relatively luxurious civilian version of the C-47, the DC-3, also served as the backbone of most 1940's airlines. Usually the largest plane in the fleet for the longest hauls, DC-3 airliners

carried hundreds of thousands of passengers all over the
world until larger planes such as the Constellation came
along.  All of these beautiful airliners were eventually
replaced by jets, but in their day prop-driven planes such
as the DC-3 were glorious.

That I managed to <u>lose</u> one of these beauties
involves several factors, not the least of which is my
generally trusting nature.  After a couple of animal
hauling trips in a re-built twin Cessna, I bought a DC-3
with my Warner Brothers money.  The airplane cost me an arm
and a leg, and I had to go deep into hock as well, but I
was very serious about importing animals.  I had my
airplane converted to a top of the line, "A-number-one,"
luxury animal transporter.  Only a fool would fail to
recognize the exotic animal business as a real profit-
maker, and in spite of what you might think having read
this far, I was no fool. Fiber glass was form-fitted
throughout the interior of my DC-3, then custom-made, bolt-
down cages were built in.  Automatic animal safety and
comfort mechanisms were installed.  My passengers could
feed and water themselves during flight with dispensing
nipples in each cage.  At the end of a flight, the entire
interior of the airplane could be washed down and flushed
out just like the deck of a fishing boat.  There was room

in that plane, and a market, for five hundred monkeys, not to mention many birds, fish, turtles, snakes and other exotic creatures. This DC-3 was one classy animal-hauling airplane and I figured to make a fortune with her.

Hell, it was so nice I should have charged the animals for the ride.

No small time, fly-by-night operation was the Hudson animal business. I had several great white hunters working full time, just like the guys you see in the movies with white teeth and quick smiles and dressed in khaki shirts with epaulets and big-pocketed shorts. They were men who were paid well to bring in and have vaccinated and ready-to-ship the young and healthy animals I needed for transport to the United States. They were good at their jobs. Rarely did they hurt an animal that would sooner or later be a beloved pet in some home in America.

Setting up and operating a company such as mine took a lot of time and effort and money, so I developed the habit of plowing profit back into the operation. Eventually, this hurt me, and although I had good equipment and staff, I always seemed to be working on a shoestring, with a regular "cash flow" problem. Still, things were going along well enough.

The animal load of two or three Vultee V1A's

could fit in the cargo bay of my DC-3 without even bumping the flight deck. Ringling Brothers would have been proud of my airplane, and my operation, and so was I. If I was going to do it, I wanted to do it _right_. Nothing, I decided, was too good for my animals. I _liked_ the cute little bastards.

It is quite possible, since monkeys are rather long-lived creatures, that somebody in the United States today has a pet monkey they love, one that is the son or daughter of a monkey I flew in on my airplane.

My monkey business was flourishing. I was making one trip every twenty eight days, and I was netting nearly three thousand dollars profit on every trip. This was a huge amount of money in those days. My gravy train was high-balling down the main line. I had an investment in the business of nearly one hundred thousand dollars, and almost no cash, but I wasn't worried. Everything was going along just _great_.

Mary and my two boys were in Saticoy, California, running a golf course known as "Charmin' Charlie's" and doing very well. I was the pro at the golf course between flights.

Have you ever noticed how, just when things are going exactly as you dreamed they would, lightning can

strike?  No reason for it that you can think of, but it
happens.  It's like fate, or some great controlling spirit
who suddenly sees how well you're doing and how happy you
are at your work and says, "Wait a minute!  We can't have
Charlie Hudson getting too fat and sassy.  Let's take a
quick shit on him!"

I was working hard, investing my money in my
business, adding to my family's security, abiding by every
law of import including vaccinations and all the other
paperwork, when it happened.  Lightning struck.

Actually it touched down far from my base of
operations, but in a roundabout way, it killed me.  There
was a yellow fever epidemic in Spanish Honduras.

"You can't unload here, Hudson," said the customs
official at Brownsville, Texas, where I normally brought my
animals into the United States.

If I knew then what I will write about later, I
would have reached for my wallet instead of discussing the
matter, but I had yet to learn that valuable lesson about
our flexible United States Customs Agents.  "What do you
mean?" I asked.  "My animals are in perfect health and they
need to be moved off the airplane.  Yellow fever in
Honduras has nothing to do with me."

"Yellow fever has to do with all of us," this

prick fired back.  You know how government workers are.
Give them an ounce of authority and they try to make it a
full pound.  He couldn't have cared less about my poor
monkeys, sweating in the cargo area of the airplane.
"We're quarantining your load where they are, on the
airplane," he announced authoritatively.  "You can't unload
them here."

I tried to argue.  The temperature in Brownsville
was always high, and inside a parked airplane on a hot ramp
it could get deadly.  My shirt was soaked with sweat, and I
was getting angry.  One thing I didn't have in the cargo
bay was air-conditioning.  The situation was quickly
becoming critical.  I tried using a softer tone of voice
with the asshole.  "Listen, my animals are suffering.  I
need to get them out of there, and I promise you they're
OK.  They've all been vaccinated, and they do not have
yellow fever."

The sonofabitch looked at me without a trace of
sympathy.  You've done business with them. You probably
know.  When certain government employees have the upper
hand, they give you that superior look, that half smile
that says, "I control the paperwork, and you haven't done
your's correctly."  Hell, I didn't know he was waiting for
something.

        "Let me talk to your supervisor," I pleaded.

        Inside, my animals were dying, one by one.  It
was already too late for many of them, all because of an
epidemic nowhere near my base of operations and a greedy
customs official.  There was no way my animals could have
been affected.  Very likely this customs agent didn't even
know where Spanish Honduras was.  All he really knew,
having not been offered what he expected because I was too
stupid to realize he wanted a bribe, was that it was in the
same direction from which I had arrived.

        He finally allowed me to unbolt the cages and
move them outside on the ramp, just so the animals remained
confined, but it was too late.  I worked as hard and fast
as I could, sweating off pounds in the effort, but if my
little passengers weren't dead in their overheated cages by
the time I struggled them out, they were dying in the hot
sun outside.  The border official finally decided that my
animals were no threat and, with a huge grin, said I could
go ahead and move them off the airport.  By then all of
them were dead except for a few birds, and they were hardly
worth the trip.

        I was wiped out.  Every dime I had was in those
dead animals.  I owed a small fortune on my airplane, and
my "profit" was gone, lying there dead on the Brownsville,

Texas, airport tarmac.  Nor did I have money to buy a new
load.  My gravy train had been derailed.

So I was down, yes, but not <u>out</u>.  I still had my
airplane, though I did share that ownership with the
finance people.  There seemed only one solution.  Returning
to Costa Rica, I began to sell off my holdings while I made
contact with a wealthy friend who owned some stores in
Mexico.  He loved to fly and he needed an airplane to haul
dry goods from the United States, bolts of cloth, ball
point pens, other such items, all perfectly legal.

We were flying in one day when I asked him, "How
is it we always get moved right to the front of the line in
Brownsville?  We only spend a few minutes and we're checked
out and free to go," I said.

He grinned across at me.  "My friend," he said,
"it is because I pay them off.  I give each agent a hundred
dollar bill for 'special consideration' of each of our
loads."

"But there's nothing <u>wrong</u> with our loads," I
pointed out.  "We're legal."

"I understand, but remember what happened to your
animals?  If you had been their 'friend,' that might not
have happened.  I merely wish to be their friend, and I am
willing pay the blood-sucking bastards to take care of my

property."

Difficult to imagine with United States Customs Inspectors? It was true. We would land and be moved quickly to the front of the line, if there was a line, and quickly be approved. We weren't hauling anything illegal, and I'm sure they knew that or it _may_ have made a difference. But I guess they figured they weren't doing anything really bad by allowing us to move ahead of others, or moving us through quickly, as they may well have felt about unloading my healthy animals if I had been their goddamned "friend." They took the money, these men who wore the uniform of the United States Government and who were sworn to guard our borders against smugglers and other illegal traffic, and waved us through. Hell, we could have been smuggling drugs or anything else inside the bolts of material.

My gravy train was no longer chugging along, but I was keeping the wolf from the door by hauling dry goods between Mexico and the United States. The regular payments on my airplane were being met, and I could see the light at the end of the tunnel. Then lightning struck _again_. We were coming in with a full load when we found Brownsville, on the United States side of the US/Mexican border, completely socked in. Fog blanketed the entire area.

There was no possible way to land at our usual base, among our open-palmed "friends."

Normally this would have been no major problem. It should have been no problem.  There were other airports who could handle us a little further away, most of them with unlimited visibility, even if we did have to wait in line for awhile.  The fact that my Mexican friend was a bit tense didn't register with me when I told him we should probably land at Corpus Christi, one hundred and fifty miles up the Texas coast, to go through customs.

"Is it possible to simply orbit until Brownsville clears?" he asked nervously, looking out the window in an apparent effort to stare down the fog.

"Not likely," I answered.  "We don't have the fuel for that.  These coastal fogs can last for hours."

"Is there no other way?" he asked.

I looked across at him.  "What's the problem? We're legal. We might have to wait a little longer to get through customs, but we have nothing illegal on board."

My words didn't seem to calm him, but we really had no choice.  We couldn't stay in the air forever, Brownsville was socked in tight, and Corpus Christi was the safest, most logical alternative anywhere near the Mexican border. We flew there and landed.

Almost immediately we were thrown into <u>jail</u>. To be perfectly accurate, we were in a nearby motel, sleeping, when it happened. The first thing I did after we parked the plane was call our pals in customs in Brownsville to tell them where we landed, since they were expecting us according to our flight plan.

"And call your buddies up here and tell 'em we're OK, will you?" I asked on the telephone. "They're looking at us kind of funny."

"Yeah, yeah, we'll take care of it," the customs guy in Brownsville responded, though he didn't sound very enthusiastic. Later I realized they didn't want anybody to know about them taking money, money they would not get on this trip in any case. "You take off tomorrow and come down here," he suggested. "We'll have good visibility by then and we'll check you through."

Seemed like a good idea to us, so we went to bed. It was our routine for me to hand over our passports to the agents when we landed at Brownsville, then they would be returned to us quickly as we were approved. Following this procedure, I handed our papers to the customs people in Corpus Christi, expecting them to be handed back when we took off the next morning. By then our friends in Brownsville would have called, and everything should be fine.  We left the plane on the ramp and found a place to spend the night.

When I walked away, I didn't dream it would be the last time I would ever see the faithful, hard-working and hard-earned DC-3 airplane as her owner/pilot.

Wheels were turning in the Corpus Christi offices of US Customs.  The customs inspectors didn't know us from Adam, nor did they ever get a call from Brownsville.  Meanwhile, what I didn't know was that my Mexican pal had a bogus passport.  Remember, this was a wealthy guy who owned stores, and radio stations, and race horses, in Mexico.  He was a well-known, upper-class citizen with a luxury home, and a nice guy at that.  People in Mexico recognized him on the street.  Apparently he had once had his passport revoked for what he insisted was a minor infraction, and one of the Corpus Christi agents recognized him.  Double-checking, the agent found that the new passport was in the wrong name.  In Mexico citizens often go by their first or given name, then their mother's last name, then their father's last name.  What my friend had done after his first passport was confiscated, was to merely save some time.  He dropped his father's name and ended his own name with his mother's name. Legal enough, I suppose, if other circumstances hadn't occurred, but Mexican officials felt it necessary to remove his passport so he couldn't travel out of Mexico to other countries. He got around this by applying for a current passport under this "new" name, and they caught him in Corpus Christi.

I knew none of this until they surrounded our motel with armed agents and finally arrested us. They booked me for aiding and abetting an alien, and according to a newspaper story that finally reached my family back home, hauling contraband and violating import/export laws.

I was finally released on bail after obtaining a lawyer, not that I care for lawyers all that much. Certainly in the next few years they would play an important part in my life, including this particular lawyer for several years to come, but I didn't know that at the time.

Nor was I released before I was threatened with a beating. "See this, Hudson," said a Corpus Christi policeman unfamiliar with my past and showing me a set of gloves with lead weights in the knuckles. "You either tell us what you're hauling in that plane, or we'll work you over _hard_."

I grinned at him. All I could think of at that moment was the worry of getting caught and tortured by the Gestapo in Germany after being shot down. Now _that_ was a

<u>worry</u>. They <u>really</u> knew how to hurt you, and although I
knew this cowtown Texas cop acting so tough would enjoy
hurting me, it was still a laugh. "You saw what I was
hauling, you sonofabitch," I growled. "I ain't gonna talk
to you even if you <u>kill</u> me, and I'd like to see you explain
<u>that</u>."

Since my wealthy friend was an alien, they held
him in jail without bail and the Texas cops did beat him
rather severely. I like to think that things have changed
now, but in those days the beating of prisoners wasn't all
that unusual in nondescript jails by "lawmen" on both sides
of the southern Texas border. This was especially true
with Mexican prisoners in a Texas jail, or American
prisoners in a Mexican jail. It was really the only
recreation the jailers enjoyed. At least one of these
latter jails was a facility I was to become familiar with a
few years later, during another crazy escapade.

The reporter who wrote the story on my arrest was
very nice after my hearing. "I feel like I should write a
retraction," she admitted. "They never once brought out
all that stuff they told me earlier, the stuff about you
flying contraband. I don't think they ever really believed
that themselves."

I demurred. "Please," I asked, "don't write any

more.  My family back home is already shook enough, and
this is going to end soon."  Or so I thought.  Ultimately
they asked me to sign a paper pleading guilty to a
misdemeanor.  If I would sign the innocent-looking
document, it would save a great deal of time and effort,
they assured me.  I wasn't really guilty of anything they
said, but this would clear the slate of any charges and
prevent further court action.  It was the best way, the
sonofabitches promised.  They would just fine me a few
dollars and what was more important, they would release my
friend to go back across the border into Mexico.  All
things considered, it seemed reasonable to me, so in what
was one of the dumbest mistakes I ever made in my life, I
trusted them.  I signed the paper.  They did as they
promised.  They fined me and they released him, but by
signing the paper I had admitted to a crime.

My friend was happy, I was not.

As he disappeared back to Mexico, I learned the
true details of my punishment.  When everything was added
up, my fine came to only a couple of hundred bucks.  What
they didn't mention before was the fact that now that I was
an admitted crook, they also permanently impounded my
beautiful airplane, probably the juicy plum the bastards
wanted in the first place.  They can do it, to you and to

me and to anybody.  Remember, I had done nothing wrong,
hauled nothing illegal.  I had a clean slate, and in fact
was a damned war hero.  But even though this is the United
States and I was a US citizen who had committed a very
minor misdemeanor offense at best according to a legitimate
court of law, my airplane was taken from me and was to be
auctioned off to the highest bidder.  The proceeds of the
sale would go to the police department and the customs
people.  The whole thing smelled like a week old dead horse
on a hot summer day, but it was happening.  I was just
sorry two government agencies in the United States,
agencies we should all respect, had to stoop so low to
survive.  But after I lost my animals in Brownsville
because I didn't know I should offer a bribe, and after my
Mexican friend had bribed customs officials for special
treatment, I shouldn't have been surprised.

        My one-hundred-twenty-five thousand dollar
airplane was, I knew, worth much less at auction, where
there were usually very few bidders on such a specialty
item as an airplane.  Often there are only one or two, in
which case the item is generally sold for pennies on the
dollar.        But wait a minute!  Just hold on here!
Being one to always look for the best in any situation, I
began to realize that this entire unpleasant matter could

be handled in a way that would make everybody relatively happy. I could get my airplane back if all went well. I would still owe fifty thousand dollars on it, but that was what I owed before. I could at least be back where I started, owning a beautiful airplane and only a couple of hundred dollars, and a little time, lost.

As any sane person might, I turned to my attorney.

Big mistake, as many sane people have learned. Especially when you leave one thousand dollars with your attorney, and specific instructions on what to do with it while you head back to California.

"Take the money and go to the auction when they finally hold it," I told him. "Go ahead and bid till you get the plane, then use the thousand dollars to secure the deal until I can get you the rest of the money." I had some money in the bank, and I figured that at a government auction, with not many people bidding, the plane might go for two or three thousand dollars at the most, maybe less.

On the day of the auction only one person was there to bid on my plane. Good news, huh? Talk about luck! By law, they'd have to accept whatever that one person wanted to bid, and there would be nobody there to raise the ante.

No, it was <u>bad</u> news, because the one guy there <u>wasn't</u> my trusted lawyer. At about that same time, in a great stroke of "honesty," he returned my one thousand dollars with a story about "forgetting" to attend the auction. Here I thought lawyers had to keep notes.

At the auction, with only one bidder, my plane went for a grand total of only nine hundred dollars. <u>Nine hundred dollars</u>, for a one hundred twenty five thousand dollar airplane! She had more than nine hundred dollars worth of <u>fuel</u> in her tanks. But she was gone, just like that.

And talk about coincidence, the greatest coincidence of all was who <u>bought</u> the plane. The winning bidder, the <u>only</u> bidder you'll recall, was my lawyer's very own brother-in-law, his very own wife's brother. How about <u>that</u> for happenstance?

Not one to take such an obvious railroading lying down, I filed suit against the attorney, with the finance company who held the note on the airplane as the very willing third party. Their lawyers weren't any dumber than me, and as lawyers they probably recognized a con when they saw it. But you know the law grinds "exceedingly slow." In three years, no progress had been made, so I signed the plane over to the finance company, which cleared me, and

they, I believe, retrieved it from the brother-in-law.  I
lost track of her, and I'm sorry about that.  She was a
good and dependable aircraft, and I hope the damned
brother-in-law didn't do anything to hurt her.

So all's well that end's well, except that for a
fouled-up passport I lost my airplane.  I was back in
Saticoy, in the golf business, looking for new adventures.

And, oh <u>brother</u>, did I ever <u>find</u> them!

## Chapter Twelve   The Great Breakout, and More

In 1972, The Los Angeles Times and other
newspapers around the country were asking questions and
making the assumptions in bold, compelling headlines.  The

interest of the press, and the public, was in a millionaire
who had vanished.

**WHERE IS JOEL KAPLAN?**

**VANISHED KAPLAN, LEFT SKEIN OF BIZARRE FACTS**

**KAPLAN CAPER, MYSTERY SHROUDS MEXICAN ESCAPE**

**DICTATOR TRUJILLO LINKED TO KAPLAN CASE**

On and on went the headlines and stories in
hundreds of newspapers throughout the country.  The story
of Joel David Kaplan was the lead story of the day in the
Spring of 1972, capturing almost every reader's attention
and imagination.  It had everything - rich, powerful
people, politics, crime including murder, and a multi-
millionaire who had apparently disappeared from the face of
the earth after a daring airborne escape from a Mexican
federal prison.  The saga had an evil uncle, a gigantic
conglomerate of companies and subsidiaries, a desperate
wife and an innocent, cute little daughter.  Not one
person, including the very rich and powerful uncle who had
helped to hold his nephew in the dingy Mexican prison, knew
where he was.

Only I knew where he was.

How multi-millionaire Kaplan got where he was is
an involved story, but the fact was, this very famous
former Mexican prisoner was a guest at my little golf

course in Saticoy, a suburb of Ventura, on the coast of California about fifty miles west of Los Angeles. He was staying in a motel next door, and hanging out with me, hitting balls and helping around the restaurant. He was my friend and welcome guest for more than two weeks, until the CIA or somebody else he trusted came and picked him up to return him to his controlling position on the board of a giant sugar company, with other branches and philanthropic arms based in New York City.

If this begins to sound slightly familiar, the whole story was made into a popular, fairly accurate and very exciting movie called "Breakout." The film starred Charles Bronson and Robert Duvall. Bronson's wife, Jill Ireland, and one of my all-time favorites, actress Sheree North, also played major roles in the movie. In fact, famed actor/director John Huston played the role of the evil uncle to the hilt.

My life had settled down and I wasn't even thinking about Hollywood. I was running "Charmin' Charlie's," the Saticoy golf course, with Mary and the boys and enjoying a peaceful existence. I did work very briefly as a driller for the Hoover Drilling Company in Ventura, just for the action, but golf was my passion. I always felt that I wanted to test the waters, to see how good I was, on the pro tour. I wanted to compete with world class golfers like Jimmy Demaret, Ben Hogan, Sam Snead, Julius Boros, Lloyd Mangrum, Jimmy Clark, and the others. I played for over a year, but by then I realized that I didn't have the real skill to compete with this class of player. My love for the game and my desire to stay on tour with these very interesting people kept me at it for a couple more years. I struggled, and meanwhile told myself that my bars would operate without me. Eventually, there wasn't anything left to operate, and I was out of the bar business.

Of course I maintained my status as a golf pro, deciding that I would be the best golf instructor I could be. That has offered me a very good living for many years. I opened a golf driving range in Ventura, and it became an immediate success and very profitable. Missing the bar business, I contacted an old friend, Bud Smith, and he permitted me to buy into a failing bar he owned in Oxnard, California, next door to Ventura. Very quickly it, too, began to show a profit as "King Arthur's." No doubt about it, I knew the bar business very well, having learned it with my first bar in Taft, the gift from the citizens of the city for my World War II service. Eventually I opened a "Charmin' Charlie's" bar and restaurant in Ventura, then

moved it to the golf course in Saticoy, where I also opened
a pro shop. We began to book several banquets a week in
the golf course restaurant, and Mary and I were flying
high. We were in clover. Life was great!

During that challenging time I also gave lessons
to several Hollywood celebrities who had learned about my
peaceful, quiet golf course just far enough away from
frantic Los Angeles. Many are still friends I see and hear
from regularly after all these years. Efrem Zimbalist, Jr.,
who says when they make a film of the story of my life he
wants to play the part of me as a young Army Air Corps
pilot and bombardier, was a special pal with whom I played
golf. We have remained in close contact.

James Garner, Joe Louis, Willie Mays, and many
others frequented my golf course in Saticoy, and became
friends. I even held tournaments on the Saticoy course and
many of my old golf pro friends showed up. It was during
that time that I paired with the great Lloyd Mangrum and a
brand new PGA professional named Arnold Palmer in a Palm
Springs tournament. I recall that Palmer was quite
nervous, but Lloyd managed to calm him down and the kid did
pretty well at golf throughout his great career.

Remember my old pal from Costa Rica, Victor
Stadter, the one who steered me into the exotic animal

business?  I'll never forget him.  He showed up at one of my tournaments, and we renewed our acquaintance.

So began yet another adventure in my life.

For after we chatted awhile, Vic broached another great idea, a plan he had for a jail break.  At first I wasn't at all interested, but Vic is persuasive so I continued to listen.  After all is said and done, I'm glad I did.

"This _will_ work, Charlie," Vic insisted. "There's these two guys in Santa Marta Acatitla Federal Prison in Mexico, outside Mexico City.  If it matters, they were both framed, and there's some real money in it if we can help them escape.  I've got it all worked out, a _perfect_ plan. All I need is a couple more pilots.

"You still fly don't you, Charlie?" asked my old pal, Vic.

I hadn't flown in ten years, but flying is like sex or riding a bicycle, once you learn you never really forget.  "Sure I do," I answered, and the next escapade began.

"What I _really_ need, aside from another fixed- wing pilot, is a totally off-the-wall _helicopter_ pilot, a screwball who will do anything for money and ask no questions," Vic explained seriously.  "This whole plan revolves around a helicopter, and a pilot who has more nerve than brains."

Vic's plan sounded like something out of a John Wayne movie, but I had been calm and peaceful for a long time. It stirred my blood to listen to Vic Stadter. Not only that, but the way Vic explained it, it did sound like it would work without a hitch. Money didn't seem to be a problem, and once they found the right helo pilot, Vic's backers would merely hand over the money to rent a helicopter and to buy two fixed wing airplanes.

"And there's one more thing you should know, Charlie," Vic went on enthusiastically. "Mexican law says that if you don't bribe anyone or hurt anyone, it's not illegal to break out of jail." I listened to him, not bothering to research the last point. It didn't really seem to matter all that much.

The first problem, Vic repeated, was finding someone who could fly a helicopter, and who wouldn't ask too many questions. I contacted an old friend, Walt Attebury, who had a helicopter company in Oxnard. He had just the pilot for me, but I spent unsuccessful weeks trying to locate him. Meanwhile, Vic Stadter was taking lessons from a young instructor-pilot in case Vic, himself, had to fly the helicopter during the escape.

Some guys can fly a helicopter, some can't.  Vic
couldn't.  When he asked the instructor how long it would
be before he, Vic, could fly as well as the instructor, the
young man looked him straight in the eye.  "Mr. Stadter,
you'll <u>never</u> learn to fly as well as me.  I'm not even sure
you'll ever learn to fly a helicopter at <u>all</u>."

Joel David Kaplan, meanwhile, had been sentenced
to Santa Marta Acatitla Federal Prison in Mexico for 27
years for the alleged murder of Luis Melchior Vidal.  Luis
Vidal was a New York Puerto Rican involved in the sugar and
molasses business.  It was a fascinating case in the United
States and in Mexico, a case that hinted but never proved
things like gun running, international dope smuggling,
espionage activities, and the possibility that the body of
Vidal was really that of an itinerant Turkish peddler.
Kaplan, the forty-five year old son of "molasses king"
Abram Isaac Kaplan, insists to this day that Vidal is still
alive and well.

"The Mexican government knows he's alive but has
refused to vacate the sentence against me," Kaplan said
from prison.  He had long maintained that it was his uncle,
Jack Kaplan, then chairman of the board of Abram Isaac
Kaplan's huge company, who was trying to keep him in prison
in order to maintain control of giant Southwest Sugar and

Molasses Company of New York, affiliate American Sucrose
Company, and the "J.M. Kaplan Family Fund."  The latter
fund was said to be a funnel for the Central Intelligence
Agency to pass money into labor and student organizations
in various Central American countries.  Since the sugar and
molasses industry deeply involved the Mexican economy,
inmate Joel Kaplan felt the Mexican government was
cooperating with his uncle to keep him safe, but solidly in
prison and out of the way.

"They sent me to prison for twenty-seven years
and even the Mexican Supreme Court refused to review (the
case) when they found (Vidal) alive," said Kaplan. He did
also admit during his murder trial that he knew and had
dealings with Vidal, and that he, Kaplan, occasionally
enjoyed a bit of minor smuggling during his world travels.

Vidal was reported shot to death and a body
identified by Vidal's "wife" as that of her husband was
found near Cuernavaca, Mexico.  Kaplan and two others were
arrested for the murder.  Although the full story will
probably never be known, Kaplan insisted that the "murder"
was a scam, a charade.  Curiously, the two men arrested
with Kaplan very soon slipped out of the country and have
never been heard from again.  Vidal, who was in trouble
with the law, helped plan the whole thing in order to

Olney 284

disappear, according to Kaplan. Kaplan and Vidal met in
Mexico City, obtained a body from the morgue, shot it
several times, then, with some bloodied clothing and other
identification from Vidal, dumped it where it was
eventually found.

According to Kaplan, the two conspirators
arranged for a slip of paper with a woman's name, Vidal's
"wife" according to the plan, to be found in one of the
pockets of the dead man's bloodied clothing.  This was done
so the body, according to Kaplan of a man much older and
much heavier than Vidal but easily obtainable, could be
"identified."  That was all there was to it.  Vidal could
disappear.  But, Kaplan insists to this day, there never
was a murder in the first place.  The body was from a
Mexican morgue, dead and cold and stiff before the
operation began.

Meanwhile, the story of the battle for control of
Kaplan's company, at that time very securely in the hands
of Uncle Jack, was well known in the business world.  By
then Kaplan had served nine years of his sentence at Santa
Marta Acatitla Federal Prison in Mexico.  From prison he
continued to say, "although I'm no boy scout, and I have
smuggled some guns in Central America, I did not murder
Luis Vidal."

What was our job to be?

Get him <u>out</u>!

Sure, I was getting caught up in the project.
Things were going well in Saticoy, smoothly though without
adventure, and although I was enjoying teaching golf, I
really wanted some excitement. Vic couldn't have come
along at a better time. According to him, Kaplan's sister
in Santa Fe, New Mexico, Judy Dowis, had offered a million
dollars to anyone who could get her brother out of prison.

Not that Kaplan had it all that bad in Santa
Marta Acatitla. You know how it was in a Mexican prison.
If you had money, you had almost total freedom inside the
walls, including the freedom to have women any time you
wanted them, or, I suppose, <u>men</u>, if you were of that
persuasion. The guards were on your side. You could pay
for servants to bring your meals and clean your living
area, and you could fix up that area like a room at home.
Since he was from a very wealthy family, Kaplan was able to
pay for all the extra privileges he wanted, including
meeting and marrying a Mexican girl while serving his time.
He could enjoy all the conjugal visits he wanted. His new
wife had the run of the place, the guards were polite to
her, and she could come and go, and see him, at any time of
the day or night. When I first met Kaplan, I learned he

had a year and a half old daughter.

"I'll admit that I'm not doing all that well learning to fly a helicopter," Vic told me one day. "My instructor, Roger Herschorn, is worried about whether I'll ever learn, so we have to keep looking for a pilot with more guts than brains."

The plan was simple and very elaborate at the same time. The helicopter, disguised as the one belonging to the Attorney General of Mexico, would land in the main prison compound. This landing was timed to occur while almost everyone was watching the prison's daily movie. Two fixed wing planes, one piloted by me and one by Vic, would be waiting a few miles away at a deserted landing strip, our command center. Two prisoners, Kaplan and a Venezuelan inmate by the name of Carlos Antonio Castro, serving time as a political prisoner, would be ready and waiting. They would be on time, since an hour before the escape they would be warned by Kaplan's wife and a man by the name of Harvey Orville Dail, who would ultimately have a profound effect on my life in another way.

There were some problems. We had to obtain the airplanes, and coordinate the timing. And we had to keep searching for a helicopter pilot. It was becoming very evident that Vic would never master the machine, and it was

far too late for me to learn to fly one of them. In fact,
we were gathering for the attempt, and we still had only
young Roger Herschorn, Vic's instructor. Roger, a superb
helicopter pilot, wasn't part of the original escape plan,
but we began to look at him seriously. Other than to fly
our official-looking helicopter to the landing site, he had
been told he would be moving some mining equipment, nothing
more. Vic was to fly Joel Kaplan to Brownsville in one of
the fixed wing planes. My job was to fly Castro to
Guatemala in Central America, from where he would go home
to Venezuela in South America. Everything was nearly ready
and word was that Kaplan was becoming impatient. We had
gathered at the deserted airstrip in Mexico, the helo
"swish-swishing" in the background.

     "Roger, how would you like to make an extra chunk
of money?" I asked the young helicopter instructor. Vic
Stadter was nodding, knowing very well that if he tried to
fly the mission he'd probably crash and kill everybody,
possibly including me, though I would be forty miles away
from the prison.

     Herschorn, not exactly certain what was going on,
paused before he answered. Then he spoke in his slow
voice. "Well, Charlie, I was told I would be flying some
mining equipment back into the hills. What else did you

have in mind?" You got the feeling he wasn't interested in anything illegal.

"Why not jump into my plane," I suggested. "I'd like to show you a very easy way to earn a very nice bonus."

He crawled into my plane, and we took off. Vic was waiting with bated breath on the ground. In only a few minutes we approached the grim, forbidding Santa Marta Acatitla Federal Prison.

"What's _that_?" asked Roger, very prophetically I thought. I mean, already he was showing an interest in our plan.

"That's a goddamned Mexican federal prison, Roger." I tried to make my voice gruff, as though I was angry. "It's a hellhole; a scummy, rotten place."

"Oh," he said, noncommittally.

I pressed the subject. "Roger, do you know how many people they have down there in that slag dump from hell who are _totally innocent_?"

He looked down again at the grim, walled buildings among the rolling, green hills, then forward, as though to the mining site. "No, I don't," he answered. "So, where's the mine?"

"I mean, totally _completely innocent_," I pressed

on. "Guys who have been railroaded into prison for <u>life</u>, Roger, who have had to leave their beloved wives and precious children." I hoped I wasn't going too far. "Can you imagine how they feel?" I slowly turned the plane, orbiting the prison.

"No, I guess I can't," he answered.

"Think how good it would make you feel, Roger, if you could <u>help</u> one of those poor bastards."

He looked down for the third time. In the exercise yard we could see inmates wandering aimlessly about, and they certainly looked lonely and unhappy to <u>me</u>. "Yeah, I guess so," he said without enthusiasm.

I pressed my advantage. "And, Roger, look at that big yard. Hell, almost anybody could set a helicopter down there without any trouble at all."

You could almost see the hairs on the back of his neck begin to stand. Color started to rise in his face. "Just what the hell are you <u>talking</u> about, Charlie? What the hell are you <u>getting</u> at?"

I swallowed, and then rushed forward. No time, I figured, like the present. Circling the prison a thousand feet overhead, I confessed. "Roger, the fact is, we're here to help a couple of completely innocent men regain their freedom."

_Freedom_ sounded a hell of a lot better to me than _escape_.

Rushing on, I said, "The two planes, this one and the one back at the strip, are for them. I bought this one with CIA money and they're going to buy it back from me after the escape. That's how sure _they_ are that it'll work, Roger. Everything has been carefully and precisely planned down to the last wave of the brakeman's hand on the last freight train out of town. I mean, down to a gnat's ass, Roger. _Nothing_ can go wrong. All we need to complete the plan is..."

"No _way_, Charlie! Are you _crazy_? I'm getting _married_ in a couple of weeks. I don't want to spend my honeymoon in a Mexican prison, or _dead_! No _way_, I say!"

"Now, Roger, calm down," I soothed. "This is going to be even easier than it looks." At that point, there seemed no reason to tell him that I was there because they had tried to set Kaplan free once before, and had been caught. The pilot they used on that attempt had been beaten severely. As the second attempt neared, that pilot had suffered a brain hemorrhage as a result of the earlier beating and ended up in a hospital, out of the plan. That's when Vic contacted me. "The only problem is, if you won't do it then _Vic_ will have to try."

"<u>Vic</u>?  Are you <u>crazy</u>?" Roger repeated.  "Vic couldn't land a helicopter in the middle of the <u>Sahara Desert</u>, let alone that prison yard down there. Hell, he'll kill himself and a dozen prisoners trying.  No way, Charlie, no <u>way</u>."

"Then you think it's impossible for any pilot to land a chopper in that yard?"

"Well, no, I didn't say that, exactly.  There does seem to be plenty of room down there."

"Are <u>you</u> a good enough pilot to accomplish such a landing, Roger?"

"Well, sure, I <u>could</u> do it.  I don't <u>want</u> to, but if I <u>did</u> want to, I could.  Vic?  He'd <u>never</u> make it."

"Then you can see our problem.  Those two poor guys down there, and one of them is an <u>American</u>, Roger, are desperate, totally <u>desperate</u>."  I was cooking along by then. I was giving it my best shot.  "The thing is, a young man like you just getting married, you could use some extra money, right?  Well, Vic is prepared to pay you several hundred dollars extra if you'll land there, wait only ten seconds, then even if nobody shows up, you take off. We rented the helicopter in Houston.  They painted it the correct color, and it has a Mexican Justice Department insignia on it.  Most of the guards will be at a movie, and

Olney 292

the others will certainly believe you're the Attorney
General, especially since you'll be in <u>uniform</u>, Roger.
They won't even be able to <u>think</u> about doing anything in
ten seconds, and they would never <u>dare</u> to <u>do</u> anything. It
would take them twenty minutes to decide that. You know
the Mexicans. Hell, Roger, they don't want any trouble.
It'll be <u>easy</u>,"

      Roger was thinking, and that was a good sign.
"So <u>that's</u> what that insignia is, huh?"

      "We've covered it all, Rog."

      He looked down at the prison. "Several hundred
bucks extra, huh?"

      I nodded.

      "Only ten seconds on the ground, huh?"

      I smiled, nodding again. By then I was turning
away from Santa Marta Acatitla Federal Prison and heading
back to the strip. No sense allowing him to dwell on the
desolate-looking place. By the time we landed, I knew
Roger Herschorn had become a part of our plan, a part we
desperately needed for success.

      The whole operation worked so smoothly even I was
surprised. Once when Roger's resolve weakened, Vic took
him aside and filled him with beer. He was soon ready to go
again. Dail told Kaplan exactly when he and Castro were to

be in the yard.  It was stressed that Kaplan and Castro had
only ten seconds to get in the helicopter, that it would
wait no longer.  Roger Herschorn fluttered in before
surprised Mexican guards and landed perfectly in the center
of the yard.  He counted the seconds in his head, his heart
in his throat, waiting for a bullet from the watching
guards, probably thinking of the woman he was hoping to
make his bride, but who he was sure he would never see
again.  Meanwhile, those guards not at the daily movie were
standing at attention on the walls.

     "One!" counted Roger, then, "two..."  He looked
around.  "Three...four..." he said to himself.  Just at the
count of "five," Kaplan and Castro came running across the
yard. The guards and prisoners in the mess hall watching
the movie "The Altar of Blood" didn't even know what was
happening.  The guards on the walls wouldn't have fired on
that helicopter for anything.  In less than a minute, the
helicopter was in and out and gone, and the guards still
didn't really realize what happened.  It was the first-ever
helicopter escape from a prison.

     In the exciting movie "Breakout," which I
recommend, it was Vic Stadter, played by Charles Bronson,
who struggled the helicopter into the prison yard, flopped
it with almost no flying skill to the ground, and made the

rescue.  Joel Kaplan, played by Robert Duvall, crawled in
and escaped, but the other inmate, who turned out to be a
bad guy in the movie, died in a fall from the landing skid
as the guards fired wildly at the disappearing helicopter.
In the movie it was Kaplan's American wife, played by Jill
Ireland, who financed the whole operation.  I think the
real life episode was better, but since Bronson did mention
"Charmin' Charlie" in the movie, I enjoy watching it, and
so will you.

The real-life plan continued to go smoothly.
Herschorn took off from the airstrip and headed back to
Houston in the helo, a wealthier, happier, and much-
relieved young man.  Vic took off with Kaplan for
Brownsville, and for a day or so I lost contact with them.
I loaded Castro into my plane, and we headed for Central
America.  Behind, we left nothing, no trace.  The plan had
been perfect.

So how did Joel Kaplan wind up at my golf course
in Saticoy, California?  And with every reporter and the
CIA and his uncle and police and everyone else looking for
him? First, as Castro and I were heading for Guatemala, he
changed my mind.

"They'll <u>kill</u> me there, Senor Hudson," he
protested.  "I am a <u>cabinet member</u> in Venezuela.  I am

<u>wanted</u> in Guatemala!"

"But the plan calls for me to fly to Guatemala City to refuel," I answered, not caring all that much about petty politics in Central and South America, "and so far, everything has worked exactly as it was supposed to. There will be people from the consulate there waiting to talk to you."

"And they will kill <u>you</u> as well, just for being with me."

That did, I admit, get my attention. "Then where do you <u>want</u> to go, Carlos? How about Middlesex in Belize?" I asked, mentioning an area I knew that was once called British Honduras. "It's right next to Guatemala."

That was fine with him, so that's where I headed the airplane. I knew and enjoyed Belize, if I could find the city and the airport in the dark. We flew on, though it was by then the middle of the night over a black jungle, with a black sky overhead. Belize is ninety percent covered with swamps and thick, hot and humid forests. There are few people in Belize. If we had gone down, they wouldn't have found our wreckage for years. Worse, Carlos, who hadn't had a good cigarette in months, kept trying to light up and I kept taking the matches from him. In the back seat were cans of fuel I was carrying for an

emergency. By the grace of God and pure luck, and a little
Army Air Corps navigation thrown in, we hit the airport at
Middlesex exactly on the nose. We came up over a black
hill and there, directly ahead, were the runway lights.

        _Damn_, they looked good!

        I landed the airplane and we then headed for the
only good food and drink in the area, a local whorehouse.
Carlos Castro had been provided an "escape kit" with
several hundred dollars and several different
identifications as a part of the original escape plan,
though he still hadn't had the opportunity to smoke any of
the cigarettes. The girls weren't that interested in the
paperwork, but they quickly got him drunk and cleaned him
of all of his money,

        The next morning he boarded a sugar airplane
headed for Panama, where he was to quietly board a plane
for Caracas, Venezuela. The damned fool got drunk again
and they threw him into jail when they heard his brags
about who he was. I was already on my way home in the
airplane. It wasn't my problem.

        After a couple of days, since nobody had been
hurt in the escape attempt, and nobody had been bribed,
Mexican officials simply dropped the matter and Carlos,
finally stone cold sober, made it back to his home in

Venezuela, where he continued to serve on the President's
cabinet. I still get Christmas cards from him today, but
that is a closed chapter of my life.

Vic Stadter, who always had the knack of entering
a revolving door behind you, and coming out in front of
you, was the one who went Hollywood, hired a writer, and
came up with the original script for Breakout. I returned
the airplane to the CIA, concluded the financial
arrangements, and headed back to my golf course, believing
the episode was finished.

It wasn't. For it was then that the newspapers,
the CIA, the uncle, and many others, were looking for Joel
Kaplan. Some wanted him dead, some wanted him alive. He
was the key to the control of his father's company. He had
the deciding vote on the Board of Directors. With his
vote, he would take over and his evil uncle would be out
for good. Without his vote, the uncle would continue in
power. But nobody knew where Kaplan was. I didn't either,
for a couple of days.

Although the motion picture insists that either
the CIA or one of his uncle's henchmen made an attempt on
his life when he and Vic landed in Brownsville, they
actually filed a flight plan for Kaplan's sister's town of
Santa Fe, New Mexico. Then they pulled that plan and

landed in Los Angeles, in Garden Grove.  Vic called me the
next morning.

       "Can you hide him for awhile, Charlie?  They're
hoping to prevent him from returning to New York to vote.
They'll <u>kill</u> him if they must."

       Why not, I asked myself?  "Sure, bring him to me
and I'll get him out of sight," I answered.  They arrived
at my place in sleepy little Saticoy early the next day,
then Vic quickly left to hide the trail.  Joel Kaplan,
subject of almost every headline in the nation and
certainly the most sought-after man in the world, was my
welcome house guest as the big hunt went on.  We enjoyed
each other's company, and hitting the ball together.  I
even gave him some tips to improve his game.

       For a few days, nobody knew Joel Kaplan was
there. Two guys did learn about him just before he left.
Two of my best friends, Harold Gregg and Bob Straughn, had
a regular luncheon engagement with me every day at the
Wagon Wheel Restaurant in Oxnard.  It seemed only natural
that I finally include Joel Kaplan.  Kaplan, who was
getting anxious to return to New York, gladly accepted my
invitation.  My two pals almost had coronaries when they
learned their dinner companion was Joel Kaplan, and that
several people were at that moment trying to gun him down.

Kaplan finally went back to New York, cast his deciding vote on the board of the Kaplan Foundation, and everything was fine again.

Olney 300

## Chapter Thirteen   Yet Another Adventure

OK, so occasionally I didn't pick my friends very well or very carefully, but you'd think a Presbyterian minister would be safe and harmless, right?  I certainly felt comfortable with a long-time friend who shall be called Rick Preston for reasons that will become obvious later in this chapter.  Rick was a minister very serious about his work and also probably the best pilot I ever knew in my life.  I'm sure Rick wouldn't mind me telling that he and his wife, Judy, are today living in quiet retirement. Judy? Yes, Rick met, fell in love with, and married my "co-pilot" in the old Vultee V1A on the initial animal hauling trip.  The flight where I tossed the dead monkeys out the pilot's window.

I had settled down to playing golf with Rick and other friends, operating my golf course and my driving range, and attempting to expand my various businesses.  My life was steady, fulfilling, and enjoyable.  My friend Rick would often fly in to Oxnard, pick me up in Ventura or Saticoy, and we would fly together to Las Vegas or somewhere else for a game of golf.  We both loved the competition of the game, and we got along just fine with each other.

Did I consider us good friends?  Once when we were walking between holes on the golf course, I complained about my cash flow.  Very quickly Rick insisted that he loan money to me.  He didn't ask how I would pay it back, but just, "How much do need, Charlie?"

"Oh, I don't know, maybe three thousand or so...," I answered.

Rick reached into his pocket and peeled three thousand dollars off a roll of bills and handed the money to me.  That's the type of friendship we had.  No paperwork, no pay-back discussion, no worry.  If you think it crossed my mind to wonder how a Presbyterian minister could afford an airplane, plenty of time off to play golf, and the quick loan of thousands of dollars, it didn't. I've always been a very trusting, non-suspicious guy. Remember, if you will, my dealings with the lawyer who eventually cost me my beautiful DC-3. If you cheat me or do something bad to me, I'll eventually figure it out, but otherwise I take people at face value.

In fact, in 1975 when I began to think about building a new golf course behind my driving range in Ventura, Rick Preston jumped into the plan.  Knowing I would need money, he pulled together a group of men who agreed to finance the venture.  A golf course started from scratch costs well into <u>seven</u> figures, so they were men of substance. Meanwhile, I approached the property owners and they agreed to cooperate in the use of the land as a golf course for a share of the profits as joint tenants.

The plan was moving forward smoothly, so let's clear up one fact right now. The only time I ever met any of the outside investors pulled together by Rick Preston was at a couple of preliminary meetings discussing the proposed golf course, a golf course that in the final analysis never materialized. <u>When</u> I met them, and how <u>often</u>, is an important fact. They seemed nice enough, and friendly enough, and they obviously had money, but I <u>barely</u> knew them. I did know the owners of the property we planned to use for the golf course, and they were of excellent character and proven honesty. They were local people of known integrity. At the time, I never had any reason to doubt that the money investors weren't the same.

There were several discussions on money at the planning meetings, a natural enough subject, but the group also discussed the size and shape, and other details, of the proposed golf course. When money came into the discussion, they did talk about where certain bank accounts were located, and how much was available in each, and about other financial details I didn't feel were any of my personal business. I tried to ignore those conversations. Sometimes they would glance around at each other as though they realized they might have talked too much. On those occasions, the conversation was then steered to other matters, but it was obvious to me that some of them thought I was learning too much about their personal businesses. I honestly didn't know anything about them, or even understand what I heard. There was no <u>need</u> for me to know or comprehend their personal business. What I wanted was for them to finance my new golf course, and that was all.

About the time of the serious meetings on forming the partnership and building the golf course, I got a call from the girl who worked at the airport where my plane was hangared. I always refueled at the helicopter station at Oxnard Airport, near Saticoy, so the office at the helicopter station kept track of my bill and my flights and other details.

"Charlie, they've been back several times to check your plane."

"What about my plane?" I asked.

"Oh, they ask questions about when it's here and when it's gone, and how much fuel you usually buy. Stuff like that."

I thought about what she was telling me. "I

wonder why they're so interested?" I finally asked her. "And I wonder who they _are_."

"I _know_ who they are, Charlie.  They left a business card."

Not one to put things off, I immediately drove to the airport and checked the card.  It was from a guy in government, in the drug enforcement administration in Los Angeles.  The telephone number was on the card, so naturally I called him.

"How come you're so interested in my airplane," I asked him very directly.

He paused for a moment, then answered.  "Would you talk to us, Mr. Hudson?"

"Sure, if you want to come here to my golf course in Saticoy."

When the feds arrived, they told me why they were asking about my airplane.  "We're not interested so much in you, Mr. Hudson, but we do have an interest in your new friends, the ones you're meeting with and arranging the big financial deal."

"Yeah," I said.  "They're going to build a golf course for me here in Ventura."

One agent chuckled.  "They can sure _afford_ to build a golf course, and _then_ some," he finally said.

"What the hell is <u>that</u> supposed to mean?" I demanded.

"We've been on their case for a long time," he answered. "We've been following them, trying to catch them. We really <u>want</u> them in the worst way."

All I knew was they had offered to build a golf course for me, and to come in as partners along with the local owners of the property. They seemed to me a pretty straightforward group of businessmen, including my friend, Rick Preston. "What kind of a case," I finally asked.

He was direct and to the point. "They're <u>drug</u> dealers."

"I don't believe it," I said.

"It's true. They make tremendous profits smuggling drugs into the United States. We've been on their case for thirteen years, but we haven't been able to come up with enough proof to indict them. When you got involved, we got on your case, too."

Quickly I made my decision. I wanted <u>out</u>. "OK, I get the message," I told the guy. "I'm going to kill this deal right now. I don't want any <u>part</u> of drugs."

"Wait a minute," the drug enforcement agent said quickly. "Don't kill the arrangement. What we'd like would be for you to go ahead with it and keep us informed about their dealings."

That wasn't me. "I'm not going to blow the whistle on these guys," I told him. "If they are what you seem to think they are, and I have no proof of that, blowing whistles isn't my style. But neither are drugs. I don't want anything to do with dope," I said firmly. "Right now, today, I don't know anything, and I don't <u>want</u> to know anything." I meant what I was saying. "And one other thing, there are some straight-arrow guys in this deal, and I don't want them hurt." I was speaking of the property owners, men I knew to be of good character. These were men I was certain would have nothing to do with drug use or drug smuggling.

Government agents, drug enforcement people, are very persuasive. They finally talked me, a good citizen, into going along with the group, assuring me that innocent people would not be hurt and guilty drug smugglers would get what they had coming to them. The agents were very anxious to catch the kingpins in the drug smuggling activities, and they felt they needed what I could learn as an insider. I had no idea at the time what was going to happen to me at the end of this deal, but throughout my life I've tended to plunge in full of piss and vinegar and hope, always figuring that everything will work out just fine in the end.  As lovable con-man Professor Harold Hill believed with all his heart in "The Music Man," there'll always be a band playing at the end.  I always figure the good guys will win before the final curtain comes down.

Although the golf course deal wasn't completely set, Rick Preston called one day.  "Charlie, let's go flying.  We'll take my plane to Vegas, pick up a twin-engine job and fly down to my ranch in Mexico for a little R&R.  You need a rest, and so do I."

We had been spending many overtime hours pulling together all the details of the golf course, so what he was saying sounded just fine to me.  We met at the airport and took off.  Landing in Las Vegas, we crawled into a larger, cargo-type airplane and headed for Mexico.  On the way, Rick leaned over and said, "I didn't tell you before, Charlie, but you know that three thousand bucks I loaned you?"

I nodded across at him, not worried at all that he was going to demand instant payment.

"Well, the guys are going to pay you ten thousand dollars just for flying co-pilot on this flight.  That means when we get back, I'll owe you another seven thousand dollars."

Seven thousand bucks _more_ sounded _great_ to me.

Olney 309

I'd been spending long hours on the golf course project,
and perhaps neglecting my other enterprises.  The extra
money sounded so great, in fact, that I didn't really
bother to ask why.  Why would they be paying me ten
thousand dollars to co-pilot a flight to a vacation?  If
you think <u>not</u> asking questions was dumb, maybe it was, but
I was doing great at the time, and "the guys" all seemed to
me to be honest and straightforward, in spite of what the
federal agents had implied.  Rick Preston was my friend.  I
hadn't been involved in anything illegal that I knew of,
and I didn't intend to become involved.  Sure, I should
have been suspicious, but I said to myself, "What the hell,
let's <u>go</u> for it."  I figured what I didn't know, wouldn't
hurt me.

        I was wrong.  Very often, what you don't know, or
<u>say</u> you don't know, can hurt you very <u>much</u>.

        My next lesson in the smuggling of marijuana came
only a few hours later. We landed at the strip on Rick's
Mexican ranch in the twin engine airplane we picked up in
Vegas.  After parking the airplane on a grass strip nearby,
we spent the day lounging around the ranch.  I was
beginning to relax and enjoy myself when, that very
evening, Rick suddenly wanted to take off and return to the
United States.         "Why don't we wait till tomorrow?"

I protested.  I was just getting into the rhythm of a
Mexican vacation.

Rick smiled.  "We have to be back at the airport
at a certain time," he explained, if you can call that an
explanation.

Workers put flares alongside the runway as we
prepared to take off, but Rick, as good a pilot as he was,
taxied off the hard surface into some sand dunes just as we
were lining up.  One of the airplane's wheels collapsed.
Rick crawled out and I tried to follow him, but I couldn't
get out because of all the stuff they had stored in behind
my seat in the plane.  Finally I kicked out a small window
and squeezed my way out of the sagging airplane.  Then I
helped them unload the cargo without paying much attention
to what it was.  To me, it was just a bunch of boxes.

With the cargo hauled away, someone then set _fire_
to the airplane.  They torched the perfectly good airplane
with the broken wheel, burning it to the ground.

Strange?  Yes, I thought so, but once again I
didn't ask questions.  Rick quietly explained about the
fire as we watched the plane burn.  It was, he said, what
they had to do when an airplane was well into Mexico and
damaged too badly to take off.  It was the routine, and it
was what they did.  Rather than getting the airplane

repaired, they burned it. So there we were, deep in Mexico
in the middle of the night, with no airplane and no
passports and no way to get back into the United States.
It could be, I suddenly realized, that we were in serious
trouble.

Unless you knew Presbyterian minister Rick
Preston, that is, who I was finally beginning to realize
was saving souls by day and doing other less inspired
things by night. As though he knew exactly what he was
doing, as though he had done it before, in fact, Rick paid
a few bribes and not long after we re-entered the United
States at Calexico. I still wasn't admitting to myself
that anything illegal was going on. I was having such a
good time, and though I didn't really know them well, I
really liked the guys in the golf course syndicate. I
guess I just didn't <u>want</u> to understand. They'd never find
me flying dope, nor would any of the syndicate ever ask me
to do so, I was certain.

My overnight R & R flight to Mexico, to Rick's
ranch, had stretched to several days, but we finally
arrived back home.

The golf course deal fell through, and without
even knowing it, I had drifted dangerously close to the
pot-hauling business.

Into my life about that time came a man by the name of Jack Evans. He was a golf pro who contacted me in Ventura and finally came to visit. I hired him to help me around the driving range, we hit a few balls together and I began to learn about Jack. He was a hustler through and through, always on the lookout for some easy money. It was almost inevitable that he would meet Rick Preston, and that very soon the two of them would become fast friends. They were off flying together frequently, since Jack was also a pilot.

One day Jack suggested I could help him.

"What I need, Charlie, is an out-of-the-way landing strip somewhere not too far away." Sure, warning bells should have rung in my head, but they didn't. As a matter of fact, I knew of just such a location, a dirt landing strip up near Taft. It was owned by an acquaintance, Rick Calhoun. I mentioned this location to Jack, and he jumped at it. "Sounds like _exactly_ what I'm looking for Charlie. Can you arrange for me to use it?"

"Yeah, I guess so, Jack. But what the hell do you want with a dirt landing strip in Taft, California?" I felt like I had to ask.

"Don't spread this around, Charlie," Jack answered softly, "but I've been working on a new invention to turn on runway lights from an aircraft still in flight, preparing to land. When you hit the 'ident' button on the panel, the lights will come on down on the ground. This will be an inexpensive accessory that will increase flight safety a lot."

Rick Calhoun said OK. All he got was a set of golf clubs out of the deal, but Jack didn't need the strip for very long. I might have given some thought to the fact that drug smugglers never use the same location too many times in a row, but I didn't. Jack arranged for workers to come in and set up temporary lights, then he would fly two or three nights "testing" them. Then they would take the temporary runway lights out and come back to Los Angeles "for more work on the system." I went out and watched one night, and the system seemed to work very well. Meanwhile, Jack and Rick had become fast friends. Jack, though I didn't really know it for sure, was flying maryjane for another dealer.

Jack would fly to Mexico, pick up a load, bring it back to California and transfer it to another airplane. Then the load would be flown on to San Francisco. The delivery routine seemed to be working smoothly, though I knew very little about the details. With the friendship between Rick Preston and Jack Evans blooming, I was more

and more on the outside, which is where I wish I had
remained. Finally, Jack Evans decided to go into business
for himself and all hell broke loose.

He was flying an airplane he told all of us he
had purchased with the money he earned flying "cargo" for
the other dealer, but on the very first trip he made as
owner of his own business, he attempted a night landing on
a levee in Mexico. He crashed, totalling the airplane and
ending his cargo business.

Not one to be daunted by an accident, Jack Evans
came to me with a plan about flying gold into the United
States from Mexico. The difference in price was
attractive, and I happened to know of a working gold mine
in Mexico with owners who would almost certainly go for
such a deal. I discussed it with Jack, and he wanted to
proceed. Jack rented an airplane from an agency at Oxnard
Airport and took off for our gold mine.

Not being near the pilot that Rick Preston was,
Jack Evans simply couldn't locate the site of the mine. So
he flew back to Tucson, called and asked me to come over
and fly back to Mexico with him. Maybe I could help him
locate the mine. He was waiting for me in Tucson with his
Oxnard-rented airplane, so we flew to Mexico. But when we
located the mine, and with me in the airplane, he

encountered some difficulty landing.  In a last minute move
that happened too quickly for me to grab the controls, he
ground-looped the plane.  One wing caught and before we
knew it, we were hanging upside down in our seat belts.
The plane was totaled.

Jack looked across at me.  "Sorry about that,
Charlie, but I can explain."

"Explain?" I said.  "Your problem is, you're a
piss poor pilot!"

Jack was chagrined.  "Now, Charlie, there's more
to it than that.  I'll explain later," he said, trying to
get out of his seat belt without falling on his head on the
ceiling of the overturned plane.

It took awhile, but I finally figured it out.
Jack wasn't all that bad a pilot, he was just using some of
his own product that day.  The airplane was wrecked.  All
we could do was walk away, and once again I was deep in
Mexico with no real money, no passport, and no apparent way
to get out.

We went through the same procedure Rick and I had
gone through, a procedure with which Jack seemed quite
familiar.  We were hauled around at night until we finally
made it back into the United States.

Jack Evans tucked the keys to the wrecked

airplane under the door of the rental agency in Oxnard with a note that said he was returning the plane and would call them later about the amount he owed them. He would send them a check, he promised in the note. The agency owner came in the next morning and found the keys, but no airplane. Naturally, he wanted to know where it was. These were people I had known for some time, but they had no idea I was involved in the matter of the lost airplane. Eventually I went in to explain to them what happened, a story I would repeat on the witness stand in 1976 as a government witness in an intriguing puzzle of a trial that involved the jail break, bribes, drugs, international conspiracies, organized crime and finally, <u>murder</u>.

<u>My</u> murder!

In fact, on a very small rise overlooking what has since become a smaller golf course that now includes a regional park and soccer fields in Saticoy, my old Charmin' Charlie golf operation now called "Saticoy Regional," there is a lonely <u>grave</u>. I'm happy to say that it is empty, nothing more than a mound of dirt from a grave-sized hole that was dug and refilled. It was dug and refilled by a potential murderer, a hit-man by the name of Alton Wayne Moore, as further proof that he had, in fact, shot and killed <u>me</u>. He had a wallet, a wristwatch, and some of

Charles S. Hudson's blood-stained clothing to prove the
murder to Harvey Orville Dail, the man who had paid for the
foul deed to be done.

What goes around, comes around, I always say.
All of them, my friend Rick Preston and Evans and Moore and
Dail and Stadter and all the others are by now much older
men living straight lives, or in jail, or disappeared, or
dead. I still play an occasional game of golf with Rick
Preston, who treated me fair and square and has remained my
friend.

The feds swept in when the Mexican police found
the remains of Jack Evan's airplane. The wreckage, which
was supposed to have been burned after the removal of
certain expensive instruments and traces of cargo,
contained incriminating evidence. At that point, my
problems really began. Among them was my suspension from
the PGA, a time off from pro golf that lasted for a year.

The funny thing was, I had the United States
Attorney all set to come and talk to the board of directors
of the PGA when they were making their decision about
suspending me. The PGA was a straight organization who had
no room in their ranks for felons. The attorney wasn't
prepared to tell the whole story to the PGA board, with
several legal matters pending, but he told me he was sure

he could say enough to get me off the hook. The day came and he was there to testify, but the guys on the PGA board were "too busy" to hear him. They suggested he come back to the next board meeting. I was paying the U.S. Attorney seventy-five bucks an hour to be there. I couldn't afford more. I tried to tell them the story myself at the next board meeting, but I also was sworn to skip many of the most revealing details because the case was still active. The PGA board members looked at each other and I could tell they didn't believe a word I was saying. They voted to suspend me.

Meanwhile, after Jack Evans got caught, the feds picked us all up in one great massive arrest. What all of us didn't know was that Jack had already turned state's evidence. They had him for drug smuggling, and apparently he had been stealing airplanes for years. He would just steal one, make a run, then burn the airplane. A real neat guy was Jack Evans. You know what kind of a guy he was? He called me after his arrest but before Rick and I and the others were picked up. I didn't know he was in custody.

"Charlie," he said with all the sincerity in the world. "I need another airplane to haul some marijuana up from Mexico. There's a nice piece of money in the deal for you, if you can you help me."

Jack Evans was being very straightforward, very honest, and if anybody had been listening, what he was saying was a confession plain and simple. It was hard for me to believe what I was hearing him discuss on the telephone. <u>Anybody</u> could have been listening. Of course I'd always suspected the drug hauling activities, but this was the first time any of them had come out and said it loud and clear. Until that minute I hadn't really <u>known</u> they were smuggling grass from Mexico into California and Nevada. Maybe this was because I didn't <u>want</u> to know, but it was true.

I didn't really know. Not for absolutely sure, that is.

"Are you <u>crazy?</u>" I answered Jack on the telephone. Of course the feds were listening in on an extension, waiting for me to further incriminate myself, but I didn't know that. "I don't want to have <u>any part</u> of any drug smuggling, Jack. Count me <u>out</u>!"

Maybe Jack tried with some of the others, too, but since they were already deeply involved, and he was prepared to testify against them, probably not. Immediately after his phone call, I was arrested. They apparently figured they had enough against me without any telephone confession. We were all hauled away to jail and

life was looking very grim and bleak, indeed, not that I
didn't have it coming.

Evans told them I was one of the ring-leaders of
the gang, and though I may not have been lily-white, this
certainly wasn't true.  The drug enforcement guys even came
to me and offered me a deal if I would testify, and to be
very frank I was thinking seriously about it.  Later, the
problem became that the real ring leaders thought it was me
passing on information to the feds, and not Jack Evans.
When they have several in isolated custody, and some of us
out on bail, it becomes very difficult to coordinate
stories. Meanwhile, Jack, who has long since dropped out of
sight, probably with a new name if he isn't dead by now,
was telling them whatever they wanted to hear.  I was the
one, Evans testified, who obtained the landing strip for
the ring, and this was, of course, true.  What Jack didn't
mention was that I got the landing strip because he told me
he was working on a night landing light system.  Some of
the gang was in jail, some, including me, out on bail.
Court actions were proceeding.

The Drug Enforcement attorneys who had been so
anxious to have me testify were suddenly conspicuous by
their absence. They had Jack and apparently didn't need me
anymore, especially since I was said to be one of the big

fish in the pool.  They simply stopped talking to me, so I
went to them.

       "What the hell's going <u>on</u>, guys?" I demanded.
"You're leaving me stranded out there. I don't want to go
to jail with these guys.  The truth is, I <u>am</u> innocent.
Maybe I should have come to you with my suspicions, but
some of these guys are my friends and I didn't want to
start rumors."

       "OK, OK, Charlie, don't worry," they finally
said,  "Just stay where you are and we'll take care of
everything." they promised.  So far, I'd managed to avoid
jail time, and I wanted that streak to continue.  When I
finally went on the witness stand, I had no choice but to
say nothing at all.  I took the fifth.  I refused to say
anything, especially anything that might incriminate me.
They finally came back to me and offered me immunity if I
would testify openly in court.  From all the other
conflicting testimony, they finally realized that I was a
rather small fish in a very big pool, a fish who didn't
really have much to do with the smuggling.  They knew I
wasn't really involved.  I may have had knowledge of
something illegal going on, but even that wasn't really
true.  All I did was <u>suspect</u> something illegal.  Most
people wouldn't run to the police if they suspected a

friend of wrongdoing, nor would they dig into the matter to try to determine the truth.

Most people would do just what I did, nothing at all. I believe this, and so I took the fifth. I simply wouldn't talk.

"OK, Hudson, anything you say will not be used against you," they declared. "You may speak freely."

I didn't know <u>what</u> to do. I hadn't planned on saying anything at all. My plan was to simply keep my mouth shut and hope for the best. Maybe the judge would see that my participation was minor, and be merciful. Court took a recess and in the hall outside the courtroom I ran into Rick Preston. Neither of us had been proven guilty of anything, so we stood there talking to each other.

"Charlie, they've got me cold," Rick admitted. "You go ahead and testify to anything you want about me, if it will help you to save yourself and get out of this mess. But whatever you do, <u>don't say anything about any of the other guys</u>. This is <u>very</u> important, Charlie. These are tough men, powerful men, and they never, <u>never</u> forget."

"Hell, Rick, I don't <u>know</u> anything about any of them. All I know about <u>you</u> is that we flew together and played golf together."

"OK, then give them the exact dates of the flights, if you can recall them. Even the ones where we just played golf. Cooperate with them. As I remember, we never even completed a shipment with you aboard, anyhow. None of it will make much of a difference in my sentence, Charlie. Get yourself out of this. You really never had much to do with it in the first place." I guess that's why Rick Preston and I still play golf together to this day, now that he's out of prison. He was fair with me.

When I went back on the stand, I told them of my flights with Preston and how we got out of Mexico by bribes. I told them I didn't know the other guys except for a couple of meetings to talk about building a golf course. That was true. It turned out some of the other guys had already testified against Rick with far worse stuff. They didn't even need what I was saying, and it really was all I knew anyhow. The old days of being a lead bombardier, and having the entire Eighth Air Force drop their bombs when I dropped mine, the days of being in complete command, in absolute authority, of being the officer who gave the big orders, were gone forever. I was a small fish in a very big, very illegal drug smuggling pool, a pool I wanted to get out of with all my heart.

They didn't really want me, or even <u>need</u> me.

But I was going to pay for what I said in court
eventually.  Meanwhile, the feds promised my sentence would
be light, that I would serve no time in prison, and that
eventually the matter would be erased from the records.  I
could return to my life as a golf pro and teacher in
Saticoy, and put all this trouble out of my mind.

Big joke, huh?  You don't put federal court
testimony against a mob syndicate out of your mind or out
of your life.  It doesn't just go away.  It stays and stays
and stays.  It never goes away until everybody is too old
to try to get even, or too dead.

It hasn't yet gone away for me, though I finally
decided to stop looking over my shoulder, which is what I
did for some long time.

The feds kept their promise.  When I returned for
sentencing, we plea bargained and I was handed three years
of probation and assessed a small fine after pleading
guilty to conspiracy.  The others all got out on appeals,
and it was during this time that Rick Preston was arrested
again for hauling marijuana into the United States from
Mexico.  He finally received an original sentence of seven
years, then they tacked on four more for a total of eleven
years in federal prison, all to be served at McNeil Island.
Most of the others were also sent away, and that is as it

should be. Bringing drugs into the United States is a bad thing.

For the last time, I hoped, and with no more adventure in mind, I returned to my golf course. Other than giving some lessons from time to time, I quietly retired with Mary. Life had been good to me, all things considered, and I knew it. I wanted no more excitement. The smaller things were bringing me far more pleasure. Money wasn't a problem and we had our health. I did get a letter from the government saying that all was forgiven and that my record was clean.

Years later, when I was called for jury duty, I learned that this was not true at all. I was still listed as a convicted felon.

But that still wasn't the greatest of my worries. There were more pipers to pay before I could finally rest.

## Chapter Fourteen    The Final Test, I Can Only Hope

Alton Wayne Moore, forty-seven years old at the time and called by the newspapers a "self-employed soldier of fortune and adventurer," was a slimy no-good sonofabitch, a good-for-nothing bum who would do anything for money, and <u>had</u>.

He did, however, in the final analysis, save my life by <u>not</u> murdering me.  Moore wound up back in jail for trying to cheat the very same government who was offering him a break in return for his testimony against another slime-ball.

Wise men say you will almost certainly get fleas if you sleep with dogs, and this is true.  For a bad period

in my life, and although I denied it even to myself, I was
sleeping with dogs.  Oh, boy, did I get fleas.

The other big league slime-ball was Harvey
Orville Dail, around fifty years old at the time of my
"murder," and, according to the newspapers of the day, "a
member of a multimillion dollar narcotics ring."  He, too,
wound up back in jail, which is truly where he belonged.
You may remember good old Harvey as the one who took the
word to Joel Kaplan on the exact time of the Mexican prison
break, though the connection is not even tenuous and has
nothing to do with his hatred of me in later years.

When these two prize packages, Moore and Dail,
met, they were both serving hard time in a crummy Belize
prison in Central America.  Moore was serving a life term
for a murder he committed and Dail a somewhat shorter term
for trafficking in drugs.  Naturally, as is often the case
with such men, they were attracted to each other and became
as close as two convicts in a Belize prison who might help
each other can be close.  Of course it's true that convicts
in any prison learn never to trust anyone on either side of
the bars, and Dail learned that even his best pal, Moore,
was not to be trusted.

Me?  Back in Saticoy, I was enjoying my wife, my
family, my friends, my golf game, my life.  The court

trials were over, the punishments handed down. I had
learned some valuable lessons, and I was a relatively free
man. Although the expungement of my record had not
occurred even though the government lawyers promised it,
nobody was bothering me. Finally life was calm. Frankly, I
was looking for no more excitement. From the harrowing
days and weeks and months of life as lead bombardier of the
Eighth Air Force through the animal hauling, the prison
break, and all the other adventures, I was finally ready
for some peace. My body was scarred, but not broken. I
was a little slower getting all the parts meshed into
forward gear in the morning, much slower in fact than the
feisty young air cadet of years before who couldn't accept
the chicken rules of flight school, but once the body parts
started to move, they still moved pretty damned well.

Hell, I was a happy man. If my life had become
calm and peaceful, perhaps a little too much so for me, it
was still in many ways a real bowl of cherries. It was
good. I even had in my files a letter from the United
States District Court probation office, attesting to my
excellent character, and only briefly mentioning "a little
trouble" I had been in.

"The purpose of this letter," it said with a
touch of redundancy, "is to write a letter of

recommendation in behalf of Charles S. Hudson who once got into a little trouble with the Federal Government on a violation of an import-export act.  He was subsequently sentenced on March 12, 1976, in Las Vegas, Nevada, to three years probation.  His probation was terminated early because of his good adjustment and extenuating circumstances as he was considered a model probationer. Mr. Hudson had been very cooperative with Federal authorities and entered a protective witness program to help the Government.  Because of Mr. Hudson's outstanding adjustment, his probation was terminated early," the letter repeated.

The letter, which went on to say that I was "an outstanding individual" and that anybody who wanted further information about me could contact the U.S. Government, was signed by a U.S. Probation Officer.  The government did finally expunge the record, but it took many more hours of effort.

I'm sure my faithful attorney, Caton Machamer, of Ventura, had something to do with the final result.  We had been friends for many years and the friendship continued until Caton recently passed away. We always had a good time referring to him as "Loophole" Machamer.  I still enjoy dining with his wife when I'm in Ventura.

Note that the official government letter mentioned a "protective witness program?" That was yet to come in my checkered life.

One day, two federal agents came to my golf course and asked me to return with them to Los Angeles. When I asked why, they were straightforward. "Somebody has been paid to kill you, Mr. Hudson," one agent explained.

"<u>Kill</u> me! But...but <u>why</u>?" I asked. I was dumbfounded. Deep in my heart I realized that things had been going along too smoothly for one who was always stepping off with his right foot, one who had a history of not asking pertinent questions, but <u>killing</u> me! Why would anybody want to do <u>that?</u>

"It has to do with your testimony in a trial three years ago. Do you know a Harvey Orville Dail?" they asked.

The name rang a bell. I thought about it and finally it came to me, the part a man by the name of Dail had played in the prison escape of Joel Kaplan. But so what? Mexico didn't care, and the US Government certainly wanted nothing to do with the breakout. That was all in the past. There was no reason for Dail to want to kill me that I could think of, especially since the escape had been a complete success.

"We want to work out a plan to save your life, Mr. Hudson," the agents explained.

That, at least, made a lot of sense to me, and I began to listen to them carefully. At the same time I vividly remembered a statement of the judge during the recent trial. He had said from the bench in no uncertain terms to everyone in the courtroom and to the media, who then reported it to everyone else, that "Charles S. Hudson better live to a 'ripe old age'," or there would be hell to pay. The judge recognized my paradoxical position. He realized that I knew almost nothing of legal value and had little to do with the crimes in question, but he also knew that I was testifying in open court against a mob syndicate. In his speech, the judge, hoping to prevent what was obviously beginning to happen, forewarned anyone who might consider killing me for testifying. Apparently his warning hadn't reached Harvey Dail.

What happened to put me on this new spot was simple. Dail had arranged for the escape of his pal, Moore, from the prison in Belize.

"I'm going to be out soon, Alton," Dail explained. "I've got connections, and I've got money, and if there's one thing I want, it is to see this goddamned California golf pro dead. He testified against several friends of mine, guys who just hauled a little grass to make a decent living, and now they're in jail, and he has to pay!"

Moore must have listened, but then grinned. "Hey, Harv, I'd like to help, but you can see my situation. I'm in this hole for life. How the hell can I help you?"

"I'm going to tell you how, Alton, if you'll just shut up and listen."

Moore shut up.

"I have friends who can spring you, OK? Once we get that done, and it'll work just fine, you'll go up to California and blow this sonofabitch away. When you get that done, you'll come back to Texas and I'll hand over twenty grand. How does that sound to you, Alton, just for blowing away a lousy songbird?"

Moore didn't have to think very long. He was in a dirty Central American prison for life, with no hope of parole. By agreeing to kill me he could get help in escaping from prison and at the same time earn himself a tidy little nest egg to start a new life in the United States. He was already a killer. One more killing wouldn't matter to him, or so Harvey Dail was certain.

Moore reached out to shake hands with his convict buddy. "I'm in, Harv, and thanks."

Dail was released, and Moore's escape was planned and executed.

Of course, I was California the golf pro. Yes, I had testified. But the worst mistake I made was to introduce Jack Evans to the syndicate, through Rick Preston. If I hadn't done that, and if Jack hadn't then gone on to blow the whistle on everybody, I wouldn't have been in such trouble.

The pure truth of the matter is, I blew no "whistle." They were making a mistake if they believed that. I never said anything to anybody about anything or anybody, except about Rick, and he told me what to say at the trail. In case anyone who is still living is interested in seeing me dead because of my testimony, I'd like to once again make clear that it was Jack Evans who was squealing, not me. I said nothing, other than what Rick Preston said I should say, and that was only about him. I really knew nothing else about any of the others or their business. I was always on the outside.

Evans was on the inside. He knew plenty, and when he learned he couldn't trap me, he told everything he knew, and then some, to the feds to smooth his own way out, involving me as he did so.

"You were on the hit list of Alton Wayne Moore,

Charlie," explained the federal agents.

"<u>Were</u>?"

"Yeah, it's the damndest thing. Once Moore escaped from the prison in Belize and made it to Guatemala, he went to the authorities. He told our drug enforcement people the whole story, that he was sprung to kill you, and that he was to meet this Harvey Orville Dail guy in a motel in Dallas, Texas, for the pay off, after the job was done.

"Lucky for you, he had a change of heart."

"So what's the problem?" I wanted to know. "If he isn't going to hit me, everything is OK, right?" I asked, knowing that since they were there, the "problem" very likely hadn't yet been "solved." Further, I had a feeling I wasn't going to like the "solution" very well. But I continued to listen.

"Mr. Hudson, we'd like to go along with this murder plan of Moore's in an effort to get Dail once and for all. We can put him away for a long time if we can catch him in the act of paying for a murder."

"Hey, that's just great, guys. But to get him cold, Moore has to kill me - and I'm not crazy about that part of the plan," I protested.

They laughed at my little joke, which wasn't all that little or that amusing to me. "Well, that would do it for sure," they agreed, "but we don't think it has to go quite that far.  What we _would_ like to do is _fake_ your death then, when Moore goes to get his payoff, we'll have an undercover agent there to take pictures and make the arrest."

I thought about the plan.  It sounded logical enough, especially when I began to think that if Dail found out Moore had betrayed him, he might just go to some other hit man and simply add Alton Moore to the register already listing my name.  It did seem to me that Dail had to be taken care of one way or the other before I could relax.  So I agreed to the deception.

Before I knew it, I was living like a rat in a cage.  Oh, it wasn't all that bad at first.  In the company of two agents, I moved from motel to motel up and down California, playing golf every day.  The first few days were just fine.  I love the game of golf, the agents weren't that bad, and we were having a good time at taxpayer's expense.  But after a couple of weeks of moving from one motel to another, and living with two other guys, and attempting to stay out of sight, it began to dawn on me that the government plan to trap Harvey Dail wasn't all that good after all.

Meanwhile, Moore had dug the grave on a rise

above my Saticoy golf course then obtained some of my
clothes, my wristwatch and my wallet.  He fired some
bullets into the clothing, stained them with blood from a
hospital operating room, and headed for Texas in the
company of a government agent who was supposed to have
"helped" Moore murder me. There he was to meet Harvey
Orville Dail.

Dail, meanwhile, was under surveillance from the
moment he got off the airplane in Dallas from Central
America.  He headed straight for the motel arranged by
Alton Moore, where the final payoff was to be made and the
murder weapons returned.

Federal agents had planned perfectly, but for one
minor little matter.  After the payoff, Dail, perhaps
suspicious, eluded the agents and escaped into the night.
He was gone and my fate, and the fate of Alton Moore, was
sealed.  We both had to disappear completely, so that Dail
or his friends would never see us again.  After all, I was
"dead," and Moore was going to be really dead the moment
Dail learned that I was still alive.  It was a confused
situation for which the feds were very apologetic.

For two hundred seven long days, and I counted
every single one of them, I remained in hiding.  When
traveling from golf course to golf course throughout

California, Nevada, Oregon and Utah became sheer torture, I
insisted upon returning home. This was agreed to by the
federal agents, especially after we walked into one pro
shop in Oregon and the guy behind the counter grinned
broadly and said, "<u>Charlie</u>! <u>Charlie Hudson</u>! How the hell
<u>are</u> you Charlie. I haven't heard from you in a <u>long</u> time!"
He clasped my hand and I realized that he was Tommy
Tomelson, a friend of mine from the Santa Maria Country
Club.

For a time they attempted to persuade me to
change my name and with my wife go away to another town and
another existence. Jack Evans probably did it, for he
certainly seemed to drop off the face of the earth.
Wisely, too, because I wasn't the only one looking for the
little bastard. The government called this their "witness
protection program." They found you a new home, and gave
you a new name, and found you a new job. It meant that
your old life was over, forever. The trouble was, I <u>liked</u>
my old life. I refused and returned to Saticoy.

For many weeks I lived in the musty old closed-
down banquet room of my Saticoy golf course. This was the
bright, friendly room where many prominent people including
Governor Ronald Reagan, eventually President Reagan, had
participated in meetings and gala banquets. Shut down for

some time, it was by then dark and cold and unfriendly. I
repaired golf carts and golf clubs, never really seeing the
light of day. Only my family, and the feds, knew I was
there. I hated it when I couldn't return telephone calls
from my friends.

Harvey Orville Dail, meanwhile, was on the loose.
None of us knew how much <u>he</u> knew about the situation. At
first, after the Dallas meeting and the bloody clothing and
other personal articles shown to him by Alton Moore and the
agent, he was sure I was dead. But then, after he eluded
the police, he could have learned anything at all. He
could have found out that I was still alive, and in hiding.
In that event, he was almost certainly after Alton Moore,
who was also in hiding, as well as me. Even the police
didn't know where Dail was, or what he knew.

My daughter-in-law, who did Spartan service after
Mary died, was partly the cause of my "coming out." At
first even she didn't know I was home, living in the old
banquet room. But then she learned about me.

"You must never mention my presence to anyone at
all, <u>ever</u>," I told her.

"Well, Charlie, I won't lie," she answered.

"What the hell do you mean, you won't lie," I
fired back. "Do you think were playing some kind of kid's

game?  These guys want me _dead_!  The feds have me in
_hiding_, do you understand that?"

"Yes, I understand, but if somebody asks me a
direct question, I won't lie about it," she responded in
what I considered to be an honest, but very narrow point of
view.

In the next few days, she took a telephone call.
As she said, she wouldn't lie.  Fearing the answer, I asked
her, "Did you tell them I was here?"

"No," she said.

I breathed a sigh of relief.  "_Good_!" I
exclaimed.  "What _did_ you tell them?"

She looked me straight in the eye.  "I told them
I would give you the message."

Fortunately for us all, Dail was finally arrested
in Las Vegas, and at that point I said to everybody, "I
need a haircut.  I'm going to the barber downtown.  I'm not
going to hide anymore."

My family tried to convince me that Dail may have
offered another contract before he was arrested, and that I
could be killed whether Harvey was in jail or not.  That
could have been true.  But you can only live in the dark so
long.  "I'm tired of living like a rat in a hole," I
remember telling them.

Dail was in custody, Moore, I figured, was being held incognito by the government, and I was suffering from extreme claustrophobia. I wanted to return some of my friend's telephone calls. I emerged from my "tomb."

The police offered me protection but only until after Dail's trail. I refused. To hell with it. I started playing golf again on my own course, knowing that I would never live like a frightened animal again. They had Dail on the charge of trying to arrange my murder, which could bring a long sentence, and on transporting the gun, my planned murder weapon, across a state line. He had brought it to Moore, then carried it back.

All the prosecutor needed was the damming testimony of Alton Wayne Moore, who had become a Drug Enforcement Administration informant, and Dail would be sentenced to prison for many years. All Moore had to do was take the stand and tell the truth, then disappear into a witness protection program. Harvey Dail would be out of circulation for a long time to come. My worries seemed over. Even a federal judge helped me out by refusing any amount of bail for Dail. He was to remain in jail until he was tried and either convicted or not convicted. The judge felt that with his past, he was still dangerous if released on bail.

You know what I say?  I say, once a crook, always
a crook. Once a goddammed con-man, always a con-man.

Alton Wayne Moore telephoned Dail's wife and one
of Dail's "business associates" a month before the trail
and offered to clam up for one hundred thousand dollars.
He offered to be silent about old Harvey, to refuse to
testify, to "forget" about the contract on my life, ordered
by Dail. The little sonofabitch was willing to betray
everybody.  He said he would flee the country, never to be
heard from again, if they would give him the money.

When government lawyers learned about Moore's
offer to sell out, they were enraged.  Moore had contacted
the other side, the enemy, and even though he had been
caught at it, the case against Harvey Dail was so weakened
by Moore's offer to sell his testimony to the highest
bidder that the government finally dropped the charge that
Dail had tried to arrange my murder.  Without Moore's
testimony, government lawyers didn't have enough evidence
to proceed on that count.

Alton Moore was convicted by a Los Angeles
federal jury on January 15, 1980, of soliciting a bribe in
exchange for failing to appear as a U.S. Government
witness.  At the same time, officials in Belize were trying
to extradite Moore back to that Central American country,

where he had been sentenced to hang at one time. His
sentence had been commuted to life imprisonment through the
intervention of David Pierce, a U.S. consular official,
then Dail helped him to escape. Finally, though, U.S.
District Judge Laughlin E. Waters sentenced Alton Moore to
two concurrent six year prison sentences and five years of
probation.

I understand he had to serve his prison term in
segregation and under a fictitious name because he had
become known as an informant. Moore is probably out of
prison by now, and my guess is he wants nothing at all to
do with me. But you can never tell about men like Alton
Wayne Moore.

Meanwhile, all they had Harvey O. Dail on was
transporting a weapon to be used in a crime across state
lines. In return for a guilty plea, for admitting that he
sent such a gun from one state to another, the government
promised to dismiss the other counts against him. Harvey
Dail was scheduled for sentencing on March 22, 1979.
According to official records, Dail admitted to "shipping a
handgun from Tyler, Texas, to Los Angeles, California, with
the knowledge that it would be used to kill Charles Stephen
Hudson of Saticoy, near Ventura, California."

That was all. There wasn't a single word about

the real truth, about Dail personally paying somebody to
use that gun to kill somebody he didn't like. Dial was
eventually sentenced to eleven years in prison on the gun
transportation charge. He is probably out of prison by
now, and my guess is he, also, wants nothing to do with me.
Obviously if something untoward happened to me, Harvey
Orville Dail, if he is still alive, will be suspect. I
guess he knows that, and will steer clear of me, especially
since he also knows by now that it was Jack Evans who
squealed on his friends, not me.

But you can never tell about men like Harvey
Orville Dail.

I've been up, and I've been down. I never
realized the very real danger of flying combat, not until
much later. I owe my life to the pilots, navigators and
experienced crews I flew with. They were the best in the
world. Many of us have had some stimulating high points in
life, and some frightening low points, and that includes
me. It seems like a hundred years ago that the Germans
tried to kill me, then, more recently, the mob tried to
kill me. Both failed. The Germans had more substantial
reasons to see me dead. I can recall one WWII mission all
those years ago, when I was the lead bombardier for a
flight of several hundred B-17's. Our primary target was

solidly socked in, and so was the secondary target.  We
turned for home, planning to drop our bombs in the channel,
when I saw an idyllic little mountain village far below.
Those folks probably hadn't even been touched by the war,
they were so far back in the boonies.

I was trained to seek out an enemy target of
opportunity if all else failed, and these folks were
Germans.  All else had failed, and in my opinion this was
certainly a target of opportunity.  I sighted, opened the
doors, and dropped, and behind me dozens of planes also
dropped.  We blasted that German village off the face of
the earth.  It was my job, what I was trained for, and I
did it.

Thomas Kerr said, "Teach me to live that I may
dread the grave as little as my bed."  I believe that, and
that belief may have helped.  I've had a great life, an
exciting life, a fulfilling life.  I had a fine wife, some
great kids...and some other "excitements."  Now I have some
fine grandchildren.

Some things in my life may not have worked out
exactly as I planned.  When Mary left after forty nine
years of marriage, I recalled the words of British poet
Robert Bridges.  He said, "When death to either shall come,
I pray it be first to me."  In spite of everything, death

didn't come first to me.

So that didn't work out so well.

Today I'm the head PGA pro in Coalinga, California, where I've met some of the greatest people I've ever known in my life. Arriving absolutely cold, I was lucky to meet Ray Elliott, John Stauffer and Bill Mouren, and by meeting them I soon knew everyone in town. I became a part of the community. I may run for mayor one of these days.

My life is peaceful and as quiet as I want it to be. I'm on the golf course almost every day, have female companions, and I still have gas in my tank. I don't look forward to the day the angels come to smooth my greying hair, but if that happens I hope it isn't some late-coming young jerk from the mob who killed me because he only read parts of this book, or some German who still carries a hatred for a war long ended. If it does happen I hope nobody else gets hurt. If you read in the newspapers about a highly decorated old "war hero" suddenly departing this life due to something other than a heart attack or happy senior citizenry, you'll be able to guess why. Nobody will do too much about it anymore, and perhaps that is as it should be.

I took my chances, and I outlived most of them.

When it does happen, as it must to all of us, I think of one more quote, if you will permit me here in the last few words of this book. This one is from Winston Churchill. He said, "I am prepared to meet my maker. Whether my Maker is prepared for the ordeal of meeting me is another question."

I have no idea where some of the ones who wanted to kill me are located today, Germans or mobsters, nor do I care all that much. The war is long since won, and the elderly contract on my life, though still active I'm told, is by now frayed and worn, dog-eared and yellow, and really not worth all that much in today's economy.

Meanwhile, I simply grew tired of looking over my shoulder. I'm too old to worry.

So I won't.

**A Final Note**

*Lt. Col. Charles S. Hudson, Charlie Hudson, Charmin' Charlie Hudson, "Combat" Hudson, died a peaceful death of old age infirmities in Michigan in 2002. He was an athlete, a pro boxer, an oil driller, a pro golfer, the top bombardier in the Eighth Air Force during WWII, involved in a major prison break, an exotic animal hauler, defendant in a drug smuggling trail, and until his final days, he still yearned for adventure. He felt he'd had a wonderful life, and his friends miss him. The author of this book misses him. But he wouldn't want any of us to worry about him. He didn't worry.*